Noodles & Rice
and
Something Nice

Golden Triangle
Chiang Mai
Chiang Rai
Sukhothai
Udon Thani
Kanchana Buri
Khon Kaen
Nakhon Pathom
Nakhon Ratchasima
ANDAMAN SEA
Bangkok
Hua Hin
Pattaya
Koh Samui
Koh Phuket
GULF OF SIAM
Hat Yai
INDIAN OCEAN
PACIFIC OCEAN

Noodles & Rice
and Something Nice

TOMMY TANG

7 LOTUS

7 Lotus Press
Los Angeles Bangkok

7 LOTUS

7 Lotus Press
P.O. Box 46700
Los Angeles, California 90046

Library of Congress Cataloging-in-Publication Data:
Tang, Tommy.
Tommy Tang's Noodles & Rice and Something Nice/Tommy Tang
1. Cookery, Thai. I. Title. II. Noodles & Rice and Something Nice.
III. Pacific Rim/Global-Cuisine.

Cover and text design by Feature Co., Ltd. Bangkok, Thailand
Food photography by Feature Co., Ltd. Bangkok, Thailand
Edit by Janet Spiegel, Sandi Arabia

Library of Congress Control Number: 2002092357
ISBN 0-9718862-0-2

PRINTED IN THAILAND

FIRST EDITION MAY 2002

10 9 8 7 6 5 4 3 2 1

THIS BOOK IS DEDICATED TO ALL NOODLE AND RICE LOVERS:

Why do people go to the gym for a workout? Because they want to be fit, strong and look good. The more you exercise, the fitter, stronger that you'll get and have tight muscles that you'll be proud of. Since you know workout is good for you, then you should give your stomach a chance to do the same. The more you eat, the more your stomach has a good exercise and the stronger and fitter it gets. No way, (I heard some of you questioning my theory) if I eat like that I will look like a couch potato, (which I see nothing wrong with that) and so huge, like a Sumo wrestler.

Well! Just hear me out. Try to eat like me. I eat as much as I want, small amounts, but all day long. I eat when I feel a little hungry and I have many snacks, including cookies in between. I drink liquid as much as I want, especially soymilk and water. I heard some of you say, "hey! I like that idea" of course, I know it is. I still eat like a pig and my weight never changed over the past 30 years. I enjoy eating; I never, ever deprive myself, if I like to eat some B.B.Q. Ribs, ribs it is, but not the whole slab. I just have 3 to 4 ribs to satisfy my taste buds. So! Do not deprive yourself; this won't help if you're on a diet. The craving for food will drive you up the wall and you'll give in and over eat, especially those junk foods. Noodles, rice and pasta (Asian style) are the main staple of Asian diets. "Wait a minute! Tommy. I thought carbohydrates are bad for you," someone screamed at me. ***Give me a break!*** If it is really true, Asian people, especially Thais will be so fat. (I also see nothing wrong with being fat, it is a personal choice). For those of you who think carbohydrates are bad for you please go to 4-5 Thai restaurants, and look around at the people who dine there and see it for yourself, how fat are they? Or should I say, "how skinny they are", especially Thais.

The key to be fit without any diets is to eat 4 to 5 small meals a day, drink alot of fluids, especially water and snack in between the meals. There are some Thai dishes that can be spicy, and you sweat from it without exercise but it's a good sweat that your mouth will appreciate.

Now! Let's Get Cooking...

Tommy

● Anceint capital Ayutthaya.

ACKNOWLEDGMENTS:

A thousand thanks to my wife Sandi, for enduring aggravation, stress, many sleepless nights, booking and scheduling my appointments, while still running the business and taking care of our two girls, Aisha and Chyna. She also pre-edited the recipes and the stories. I don't really know how she did it but somehow she got it all done beautifully. I had the easy part writing it, but she really is the heart and soul behind the book. So, the words thank you to her seem pale. I am grateful from the bottom of my heart for what she has done.

Thanks to Alfonse Ruggiero Jr. and Karen Schuler, for allowing me to use your great house and its wonderful kitchen in Buffalo, New York, to write this book.

Thank you, as well, to Alfonse Ruggiero, Sr. and Joyce, who drove me around in search of recipe ingredients and tasted all the dishes.

Thanks to Feature Co., Ltd. Pi Yong, Nim, their team of photographers, and everyone at Feature, especially Pi Juke (Payom Valaiphatchra) for the creativity that has made this book come alive, and you're right, we can do it.

Thanks to Tourism Authority of Thailand, (TAT) additional photos.

Additional location photos by Keith Tianchairoj and Karen Schuler.

I spent ten days at The Rose Garden Aprime Resort, outside Bangkok, to shoot the photos and I didn't want it to end. Thanks to chef Wanwipa Bandit and the kitchen staff for helping me to prepare the foods and make sure that my photographer's teams were well fed and that I had my hot coffee in my mug. The management team, Khun Danai Wansom, Heribert Gaksch, Santana Charoenpongse and especially Khun Suchada Yuvaboon, (Pi Tew´) and everyone there made me feel at home.

Thanks to Khun Amnart Klanprachar for his wonderful painting.

Thanks to my daughters, Aisha, 15, and Chyna, 12, my wife, Sandi, Janet Spiegel, Joanne Durfee, Linda K. Mundel, and Tom Merklinger for story contributions.

Without Mr. Ma, at Guangzhou Tourism Bureau, and Yaying Li, at China National Tourist Office, Los Angeles, I would never have known the birthplace of rice noodles.

Thanks to my kitchen staff, for assisting me with testing the recipes. To all my friends and patrons who frequent and support Tommy Tang's Restaurant and always ask, "when will the book be done?" here it is. Thanks to you all from the bottom of my heart.

Thanks to my dear friend Janet Spiegel who put her own book project aside and spent less time with her husband, Dennis, to edit my book. She spent many hours making sure the text flows and the recipes are easy to follow. I will miss Saturday noodle lunches while we went over the recipes and will also miss shopping around in Thai markets for fresh ingredients to prepare the recipes at home. Without her this book would have taken much longer to publish. I am so thankful for her hard work editing this book and making it the most fun cookbook to read.

● "*A Grain of Rice*" oil painting by Amnart Klanprachar.

A WORD FROM TOMMY:

I have three wishes to make before I leave this planet called Earth and here goes:

1. I wish for a day, organized the world over, when every single person would plant 10 trees and turn this planet green again — to recreate forests to reduce global warming, produce important medicinal plants, and revive the natural habitat to save the Thai elephant and many other endangered species.

2. I wish for an international festival, like the Olympics, dedicated not to sports, but to the elimination of hunger.

3. I wish all humans could look upon each other as if they were young children, before they learned to separate, demean, or hate other groups of human beings.

The third wish is the one that I have been wishing for all my life. Now, close your eyes and let us imagine we are sitting down in a large circle. Imagine there are many children crawling all over inside the circle, children with different ethic backgrounds and skin colors, black, brown, white and yellow. Children with parents of all different religious beliefs, Buddhism, Christianity, Hinduism, Judaism or Islam, to name just a few. They are playing together without thinking who, what or where their playmate came from. They are having great happy times. They are laughing, screaming and making sounds only children understand. Sometimes they fight, but then they go back and hug each other and the fun resumes. Somehow they have a special ability to solve their differences in a civilized manner. This is because they behave and react with the pure, clean brain cells they were born with, untouched by the artificial separation of our teaching. The sounds of children laughing subside and now you may open your eyes. Welcome back to the real world.

When the children get older, they learn how to love, hate, build and destroy. They learn to separate those happy children inside the circle by their skin color and religious beliefs. We teach them that. Now, you can see what I am trying to tell you. We have learned so much through the centuries but we have learned nothing at all. After thousands of years, how could we still judge people by their ethnic background, the color of their skin, and their religions? We humans have progressed so much in technology but we are delinquent in compassion.

There is so much hate, violence, and destruction in this world that we are a part of. When is it going to end, what will it take before we wake up? We are here on this earth for a very short time and we still can't get along. No matter who you are, rich or poor, your religious or ethnic background, when you're born you will grow, get old, sick, and end the same way.

Let me tell you why my third wish is not my first wish, because I believe that we all can change and learn to get along and be more compassionate to all humankind. All we have to do is trust the pure brain cells that we were born with to bring us to a happy peaceful existence. The choice is yours and I can only wish.

Tommy

A giant guarding The Emerald Buddha Temple, Bangkok

INTRODUCTION:

You know the feeling. You've just had a meal in a nice restaurant, or even at home. You stuffed your face, but yet feel that something is missing and you are still not satisfied. You want more food. No, you want something sweet. Ah, now you're talking, the brain says to the tongue, "Here, eat this cake!"

This is what happens when your tongue and brain are not making peace. The brain starts nagging the tongue, "I'm not happy, I'm not satisfied, give me something else, something that will really make me happy." Then your tongue savors the dessert, signals the brain that now it is satisfied, and ready to sign a peace agreement. So you may ask, what does all this mean?

The fact is, no matter how much you have eaten, if the food is not tasty enough, your brain will tell the tongue it isn't satisfied. After traveling all over the world and meeting many people along the way, I find myself frequently asking people, what do you eat at least once a week, that makes you really happy? The overwhelming response has been, noodles, pasta, or rice. People just can't seem to get enough of these dishes. Every style of cuisine has its versions. They are every culture's soul or comfort food. It comforts the soul. And the tongue. And the brain.

But in my humble opinion, there just aren't yet enough really interesting and exciting recipes out there to fill the needs of these hordes of noodle & rice lovers. That's the reason I've created this simple collection of noodle & rice recipes from my homeland and around the globe. Thai food uses the principle that each dish should contain flavors that are sweet, salty, sour, spicy, and may I add sensational. I've combined the East/West ingredients and techniques to create my style of these delectable flavors. They will satisfy your taste buds because they are brimming with a combination of delicious tastes.

I have designed these recipes to suit the American kitchen and for people who have minimal kitchen utensils. You don't need to rush out and buy expensive pots and pans, whatever you have will do, but if you have state-of-the-art equipment that will be great too. I love to buy cookware instead of buying clothes. I own many beat-up sauté pans and my food turns out just fine. The recipes in this book are quite easy to follow and prepare, some may be a little harder but if you keep on cooking you'll master them in no time at all. Recipes are a guideline for you. If you would like to substitute some ingredients, be my guest, and if you create some wonderful recipes, please send them for me to try. This book has more than just noodles and rice; it includes appetizers, soups, salads, pastas and something nice. One thing you can be sure of is that it will be so delicious your brain and tongue will live in peace.

Have fun

Tommy

Contents

● Chao Praya river.

APPETIZERS

Bangkok is the fourth and present capital of Thailand. The Chao Praya River is also known as "The River of Kings." This waterway was the main transportation in the past and is still the best way to travel today. It took four major rivers, Ping, Wang, Yom and Nan from the northern part of Thailand to form and merge at Nakorn Sawan province to become the mighty Chao Praya River. The river runs through many provinces and along the way brings prosperity wherever it passes.

When you're visiting Bangkok, there are many places to see and visit, but what I like to do when I arrive in Thailand is take it easy the first day, and I also like to have a traditional Thai massage to get rid of jetlag. In the afternoon I will go on a boat ride along the Chao Praya River and canals (Bangkok has many canals). The boat ride will relax you, release your stress and allow your body to adjust to the climate of Bangkok and prepare you for the adventure. Please don't try to do too many activities in one day; after all, I don't want you to become exhausted. Just let the first day be your Bangkok appetizer.

The next day, after breakfast, you should visit the Grand Palace, and the Emerald Buddha Temple, adjacent to the Grand Palace. Across the Chao Praya river is Wat Arun (Temple of Dawn), Thonburi, which used to be Siam's third capital and Siam is what Thailand used to be called. Next, visit Chinatown, which is close by, and while you're there, you should try some Dim Sum and visit the Golden Buddha Temple. The golden Buddha weighs about 11,025 lbs. My other favorite places are the Golden Teak Palace, Ayutthaya, (the second ancient capital) and Bang Pa In Summer Palace, just to name a few.

There are many restaurants in Bangkok, and if I tried to name them all, it would take half of this book. My favorite is to venture out in the streets of Bangkok, and try the street vendor foods. You can't imagine how many varieties of foods are out there. It will take months before you try them all. I love it when I discover some unusual dish, which I can't find when I go to the restaurants. I probably can eat all day long and try every item that is in front of me. There are no other cities like Bangkok where you can find street food vendors 24/7 all year round. Bangkok is definitely a foodie's heaven! You should do it in the evening when it's a bit cooler. When you try street foods, make sure to order cooked hot foods and avoid cold foods that have been sitting there for a long time, and drink only bottled or canned beverages. Did I mention fruits? Yes! Of course, you should try all tropical Thai fruit; my favorites are Rambutan, Mangosteen, Pomelo, Jackfruit (Kar-n'oon in Thai), Durian (stinky fruit), Sa-Lha, Larng-Sard, Long-Gong, Lum-Yai, and especially Mango. If you try mango in Thailand, it will be hard for you to eat mango again, because these mangos are the best in the world and how could you top that!

Tommy

Angola Mistake

I was walking in a circle in my friend's kitchen in Angola, near Buffalo City, NY. I wanted to create an appetizer, but I didn't know what to make. I felt like a fox in a cage that wants to hunt, but with no place to go. I looked around the kitchen, opened the fridge and saw a couple pounds of fillet. But that's for another recipe I have in mind. Ah! There is ground chicken waiting for me to do something with, but I think Buffalo meat would be more appropriate. Yeah, I think I can make chicken taste and look like buffalo meat. When my friend said, this is delicious but what is this mystery meat, I said this is called Angola Mistake and tastes like Buffalo meat on the lake...

❖ *Recipe serves 4*

- 1 tablespoon virgin olive oil
- 8 oz. finely minced raw chicken breast
- $^{1}/_{4}$ teaspoon sea salt
- 4 tablespoons lemongrass stock (see page 196 for instructions)
- $^{1}/_{3}$ cup chopped pitted black olives
- 3 tablespoons red wine vinegar
- $^{1}/_{3}$ cup steamed Thai black rice (see glossary and cooking instructions, page 192)
- 1 teaspoon toasted coriander seeds cracked
- 1 teaspoon toasted yellow mustard seeds
- 1 teaspoon Kee Noo chili flakes (see glossary page 202)
- $1^{1}/_{2}$ tablespoons Thai fish sauce seasoning
- 2 tablespoons lime or lemon juice
- 1 teaspoon sugar
- 2 tablespoons small diced red bell pepper
- 1 cup *caramelized red onion
- $^{1}/_{2}$ tablespoon virgin olive oil
- $^{1}/_{4}$ cup *roasted whole rice
- 2 tablespoons toasted sesame seeds
- $^{1}/_{4}$ cup thin sliced scallions
- 2 tablespoons chopped sage
- 1 bunch mixed fresh herbs, sage, Thai or regular basil, mint, cilantro, Italian parsley, Meng Luck basil, Oba leaves or any herbs that you prefer
- 1 bowl mixed lettuces, romaine, cabbage, endive, raddicio

Place olive oil, chicken, sea salt and lemongrass stock into a small saucepan over high heat, stir for 3-4 minutes. Add chopped black olives, wine vinegar and black rice and stir for 3-4 minutes. Add remaining ingredients (except the mixed herbs and lettuce) and mix it thoroughly. Remove to a serving plate and serve with fresh herbs and lettuce.

*To make caramelized onion: place red onion and olive oil into a skillet over medium heat and stir occasionally for 10-12 minutes or until onion becomes soft and caramelized. Remove and set aside.

*Roasted whole rice: place rice in a small skillet over low heat and stir occasionally for 20 to 25 minutes or until rice turns golden brown. Be attentive near the end so you don't burn it. ❖

Beer Batter Shrimp with Mango Salad

***W**hen I experimented with this recipe, I wanted to find a sauce that would complement this crispy shrimp. I made several different dipping sauces, but I wasn't satisfied with the results. I saw a green mango on the kitchen table, waiting for me to notice it. So now the mango has the attention it deserves and I thought "why not mango?" The mango jumps for joy and here is Beer Batter Shrimp with Mango Salad.*

❖ *Recipe serves 4*

Beer Batter

- 16 medium fresh large shrimp (size 21-25 per lb.) shelled and deveined
- 1 cup sifted rice flour
- 1/2 cup sifted all-purpose flour
- 1 teaspoon sea salt
- 1 teaspoon sugar
- 1 tablespoon vegetable oil
- 1 cup ice-cold Singha beer
- 6 cups vegetable oil for deep frying

Mango Salad

- 3 tablespoons Thai fish sauce seasoning
- 2 1/2 tablespoons lime juice or lemon juice
- 1/2 tablespoon palm sugar or honey
- 1/4 tablespoon thinly diced Kee Noo chili or substitute with Serrano chili
- 1 tablespoon finely chopped garlic
- 1 tablespoon roasted chili paste
- 1/2 cup Thai long beans or string beans cut into 1- inch pieces
- 1/4 cup crushed roasted unsalted peanuts
- 1 large green or semi-ripe mango, thinly julienned
- 1/2 cup sliced red onion
- 1/2 cup diced tomatoes

Place fish sauce, lime juice, palm sugar, Kee Noo chili, garlic and roasted chili paste into a bowl and mix thoroughly. Add remaining ingredients and squeeze salad mixture with your hand until thoroughly blended. Transfer mango salad to a large platter and set aside.

Place oil into a deep skillet over medium heat (325°F. - 350°F.). Combine beer batter ingredients in a bowl and mix thoroughly. Add shrimp, and then toss until it is thoroughly coated. Place shrimp into the hot oil (small amount at a time) and fry for 3-4 minutes or until it turns golden brown and crispy. Remove cooked Beer Batter Shrimp to a pan lined with paper towels to remove excess oil. Arrange Beer Batter Shrimp around Mango Salad.❖

Dancing Shrimp

This recipe may look and sound difficult, but trust me. Yes; that's right, trust me! It is worth the time you spend to make it. All your friends will dance with joy while they're watching the shrimp dance up and down as you serve them

❖ *Recipe serves 8*

Stuffing

- 6 oz. ground chicken breast
- 1/4 cup shredded coconut
- 1 teaspoon finely chopped garlic
- 1 teaspoon granulated garlic
- 2 tablespoons finely chopped cilantro
- 1 teaspoon ground white pepper
- 2 teaspoons Thai fish sauce seasoning
- 2 teaspoons light soy sauce
- 3 tablespoons finely diced brown onion
- 1 egg white only
- 1 tablespoon cornstarch

- 24 medium fresh shrimp shelled and deveined
- 24 10-inch bamboo skewers
- 2 packs fresh egg noodles (the size of angel hair pasta)
- 6 cups vegetable oil for deep frying
- 8 cups water

Sauce

- 1 whole pineapple
- 1 cup sour cream or yogurt
- 1 can coconut milk
- 2 whole ripened mangos
- 1 1/2 tablespoons palm sugar or sugar

Combine ground chicken, coconut, garlic, cilantro, white pepper, fish sauce, light soy sauce, onion, egg white and cornstarch in a bowl. Mix ingredients thoroughly and set aside.

Thread the shrimp on bamboo skewers, threading from the tail through the head. With a small knife, score the back of the shrimp deep enough that you can flatten them but make sure the shrimp won't fall off the skewer. Place a small amount of stuffing mixture on the back of the shrimp and press gently to allow stuffing to stay on the shrimp. Repeat until finished.

Place water in steamer pot with a shallow tray and bring water to a boil. Place the stuffed shrimp on the steamer tray and steam for 4 to 5 minutes. Remove to a paper towel to absorb excess liquid and let them cool.

With a sharp knife, cut pineapple crosswise 1/3 from the top (do not measure from the leaves). With a small knife and a large spoon or melon-ball cutter, cut and scoop out pineapple meat and set aside in a bowl. While scooping out pineapple, make sure not to puncture pineapple shell. Place pineapple meat, sour cream, mango and palm sugar into a blender and blend until sauce becomes smooth. Remove and pour the sauce into the cored pineapple and close with the pineapple top.

Open a pack of egg noodles, unfold and arrange the strands on a baking tray. Hold steamed shrimp stick with one hand flat against a few strands of noodles. With the other hand, spin the stuffed shrimp around until shrimp stick is fairly covered with noodles. Press the end of the noodle strands gently into the stuffing to hold noodles in place while deep-frying. Repeat with remaining shrimp and noodles.

Heat the oil in a deep skillet over medium heat, 300°F. to 325°F. Add 2 wrapped shrimp sticks at a time to the hot oil and fry for 1 to 1 1/2 minutes. Remove shrimp sticks to a tray with paper towels to remove excess oil. Repeat until all wrapped shrimp are done. Arrange fried shrimp sticks into and around the pineapple that holds the sauce.

Now let the dance begin. ❖

Buer Tod with Sweet Tamarind Chili Sauce

This southern style shrimp tempura is a favorite among the people of the Southern provinces of Thailand. Every time I visit Phuket Island with a group of my friends, I always brought them to my favorite local seafood restaurant on the beach. When I say "local" that means this restaurant is mostly visited by local residents who live on Phuket Island, and there are not many tourists there. I love the way they use local edible grass and tree leaves dipped in spicy batter and fried. Maybe because the batter is spicy is why I like it so much and can't wait to go back for some more.

❖ *Recipe serves 6 to 8*

- 1 lb. small fresh shrimp (size 60 per lb.) shelled and deveined
- 3 cups sifted rice flour
- 2 tablespoons red curry or panang curry paste
- $2^{1}/_{4}$ cups ice-cold water
- 2 teaspoons salt
- 2 teaspoons sugar
- $1^{1}/_{2}$ cups Ya-Chong wild grass (substitute with scallions cut 5" to 6" in length)
- $2^{1}/_{2}$ cups Bai-Cha-Plu (substitute with spinach or collard green leaves)
- $1^{1}/_{2}$ cups Bai-Leb-Krut (substitute with Frise lettuce)
- 8 cups vegetable oil for deep frying

Sauce

- 2 tablespoons crushed red chili paste (Sambal Oeleck)
- 1 tablespoon finely chopped garlic
- 1 cup tamarind juice (see instructions on page 197)
- 4 tablespoons palm sugar, coconut sugar, granulated sugar or honey
- 2 teaspoons sea salt
- 1 cup water

Place dipping sauce ingredients into a small stockpot over medium heat and bring to a boil. Reduce heat to low and simmer for half an hour or until sauce becomes syrupy. Remove and let it cool.

Place oil into a deep stockpot over medium high heat (325°F to 350°F). Combine tempura ingredients in a bowl and mix thoroughly. Add vegetables and shrimp, and then toss until they are thoroughly coated. Place shrimp and vegetables into the hot oil a small amount at a time and fry for 3-4 minutes or until they turn golden brown and crispy. Remove cooked tempura to a pan lined with paper towels and serve with sweet tamarind chili sauce.❖

Grilled Mixed Peppers and Black Olives

For those of you who love spicy snacks, you will go crazy with this simple recipe. You can use any variety of chili that you prefer, serrano, jalapeno, Anaheim, Italian, banana, or Holland, just to name a few. I make this snack more intense by adding Kee Noo chili. Add palm sugar to soothe the good pain from the heat. If you feel that water is not enough to put out the fire in your mouth, may I suggest a good Thai beer? Singha beer is **my** *choice and is Thailand's first beer.*

❖ *Recipe serves 1 to 4*

- 1/2 lb. mixed chili peppers, seeded
- 10 large cloves garlic, skin intact
- 1 12-16 oz. jar pitted black olives
- 3 tablespoons extra virgin olive oil
- 1 1/2 tablespoons balsamic vinegar
- 3 whole Kee Noo chilies
- 2 tablespoons palm or coconut sugar or brown sugar
- 2 teaspoons sea salt

Place chilies and garlic on a pre-heated grill and grill until soft, about 8 to 9 minutes. If you don't have a grill you may place ingredients in aluminum foil and wrap them tightly several times. Place wrapped chilies and garlic on a wire rack over a low heat burner.

Place soft chilies and garlic into a mixing bowl. Add black olives, virgin olive oil and balsamic vinegar and set aside.

Place Kee Noo chilies, palm sugar and sea salt into a mortar and pound with pestle until smooth. Add pounded mixture to grilled chilies and garlic and black olives. Stir until ingredients are thoroughly mixed and it's ready to be eaten as a snack. ❖

> *Thai people love snacks. We eat snacks all day long and it is part of our life and culture. When we talk about snack foods, it doesn't mean just potato chips, popcorn, and cookies. Thai snacks may include all that, even though they're not really part of the Thai repertoire. Everywhere you go in the Kingdom, you will find many varieties of snacks, from sweet or sour to peppery hot. My favorite is a street fruit cart vendor, and I love pickled olives with Kee Noo chili and palm sugar. They taste so good together. Now all you have to do is go to Bangkok, see it for yourself and snack away all day.*

Golden Threads

Food has always played an important part in Thai culture and each occasion has its own dishes. When a couple gets married, their parents will plan a wedding reception menu, and all the dishes that they are going to serve for the happy couple and their guests must have some great meaning and sound prosperous. This dish is one of the favorite appetizers for a Thai wedding ceremony. The long noodle strand represents the long life of the marriage. The golden ball nugget represents wealth and happiness but that is a separate story altogether. If you are marrying a lazy person, I don't think the golden ball nugget would do any good.

❖ *Recipe for 6-8*

- 8 oz. Asian long noodles (*dried or fresh wheat noodles)
- 1 cup minced chicken
- 3 roots cilantro (substitute with cilantro stem)
- 1 teaspoon whole white peppercorns
- 2 teaspoons finely chopped garlic
- 1 tablespoon light soy sauce
- 2 teaspoons roasted sesame oil
- 1 tablespoon corn flour or all purpose flour
- 2 cups vegetable oil for deep frying
- 1/4 cup seracha chili pepper sauce

Pound together cilantro root, white peppercorns and garlic with mortar and pestle until it becomes pasty and transfer to a mixing bowl. Add minced chicken, soy sauce, sesame oil and corn flour and mix it thoroughly. Form a small amount of the chicken mixture into a little round ball, about one inch around. Wrap the noodles around each ball, a few strands at a time, until each ball is completely wrapped, and repeat the process. Deep fry the wrapped balls in medium hot vegetable oil (300°F to 325°F), until golden and the noodles turn crispy. Serve with Seracha chili pepper sauce.

***I**f you use dried noodles, soften noodles in hot water for a few minutes, drain and mix in a small amount of vegetable oil to keep strands apart. ❖

● Grand palace, Bangkok.

Khao Tang-Naa Tang Crispy Rice Cakes with Sweet Curry Shrimp Sauce

This is an old recipe that has been a favorite with many Thais in the past and is still one of the favorite appetizer dishes today. Of course, it's also my favorite too. I love the combination of crispy rice, tasty chicken, shrimp and chili dipping sauce. When you are spreading the sticky rice on the baking tray, you should have a pair of gloves handy or you can wet your hand with lukewarm water before you start. Otherwise sticky rice will stick to your hand. That's why they call it sticky rice!

❖ *Recipe serves 4 to 6*

- 4 cups cooked sticky rice (see page 191 for instructions)
- 1 tablespoon salt-free Thai seasoning
- 2 tablespoons black sesame seeds
- 1 teaspoon sea salt
- 3 cups vegetable oil

Dipping sauce

- 1 can (14 oz.) coconut milk
- $^1/_2$ tablespoon red curry paste
- $^1/_2$ cup finely minced chicken
- $^1/_2$ cup finely minced shrimp
- 1 tablespoon palm sugar or honey
- $1^1/_2$ tablespoons Thai fish sauce seasoning
- $^1/_4$ cup diced tomatoes
- $^1/_4$ cup ground roasted unsalted peanuts
- 2 tablespoons minced shallots
- 3 tablespoons sliced cilantro leaves (substitute with flat leaf parsley)

Combine cooked sticky rice, Thai seasoning, sesame seeds and sea salt and spread evenly on a baking tray. Transfer the tray to a preheated oven at 200 F. and bake for 1 hour. Turn off oven and keep dried sticky rice on tray in oven until cooled. Break dried sticky rice into small bite-size pieces.

Place vegetable oil into a deep skillet over medium low heat about 300°F to 325°F. Add dried sticky rice to hot oil and it will pop up very quickly. Remove crispy rice to a paper towel to remove excess oil and let it cool.

Place coconut milk, curry paste, chicken and shrimp in a small skillet over medium heat and stir for 2 to 3 minutes. Add palm sugar, fish sauce and tomatoes and stir for 2 minutes. Add peanuts and shallots and bring sauce to a boil. Reduce heat to low and simmer for 3 to 4 minutes. Remove to a serving sauce bowl. Add cilantro leaves on top of sauce and serve at room temperature with crispy rice. ❖

I had a chance to try this savory dish when I was a teenager and the flavors are in my fond memory. And later I always ordered it whenever I visited a restaurant that served it. I tried to keep score to see which restaurant did the best. One day, while visiting Bangkok with my television crew to tape our cooking series, I was invited to my dear friend Aunty's house and she made this for us. I have stopped keeping score; I think her style is the best, but I still enjoy them at other places, too.

Mee Krob Noodles

***I** added this recipe at the last minute. I felt something was missing. Because this dish is quite sweet, Thai people don't eat this as a main dish, but as a snack. I like to put a small amount of sweet crispy Mee Krob on a leaf of Belgian endive. The contrast between the bitter flavor of endive and sweet crispy noodles creates an explosive sensation in your mouth.*

❖ *Recipe serves 4 to 6*

- 2 oz. Crispy Mee Krob noodles (see page 193 for instructions)
- 1 cup small shrimp; shelled deveined and diced
- 2 cups fresh water

Sauce

- 2 tablespoons olive oil
- 1/2 cup tamarind juice (see page 197 for instructions)
- 1/4 cup rice vinegar
- 1/4 cup honey or white sugar
- 1 1/2 tablespoons Thai fish sauce seasoning
- 1 teaspoon paprika
- 1 whole egg, beaten

Topping

- 2 cups fresh bean sprouts
- 1/4 cup toasted slivered almonds (optional)
- 2 tablespoons thinly sliced pickled garlic (optional) (see glossary page 192)
- 1/4 cup thinly julienned leeks
- 1/4 cup sliced cilantro leaves

Place water into a small pot and bring to a boil. Add diced shrimp and cook for 2 minutes or until shrimp turn pink. Remove, drain and set aside.

Place olive oil in a large skillet over high heat. Add tamarind juice, rice vinegar, honey, fish sauce, and paprika and boil for 3 to 4 minutes. Reduce heat to medium, add egg and stir gently until blended. Reduce heat to low and simmer sauce until the mixture is thick and syrupy (about 15 to 17 minutes). Remove from heat, add cooked shrimp and let the sauce cool down to lukewarm. Add crispy noodles a handful at a time and toss gently. After noodles are thoroughly coated with the sauce, transfer to a large serving platter. Toss remaining ingredients over sweet crispy Mee Krob.❖

Rice Croquettes

There are many varieties of Rice Croquettes, each country's cuisine has its own version. I love the little rice ball. Actually they come in different shapes; squares, triangles, and of course a round ball. I enjoy eating them all. Some are stuffed with meat, vegetables, and cheese, or with a sweet bean paste.

❖ *Recipe makes 10-12 Rice Croquettes, 2-$2^{1}/_{4}$ inches round*

3	cups cooked Thai sticky rice (see page 191 in easy recipe section)
$1^{1}/_{2}$	tablespoons finely chopped cilantro leaves
$^{1}/_{2}$	teaspoon sea salt
6	tablespoons grated Parmesan cheese
1	tablespoon Thai seasoning
1	whole egg

Stuffing

$^{1}/_{2}$	cup finely diced smoked ham, Prosciutto or smoked turkey
1	cup finely diced Asiago cheese
2	tablespoons crispy roasted garlic (see page 192 for instructions)
1	tablespoon finely sliced cilantro leaves
2	teaspoons cracked black pepper
2	cups fine dry breadcrumbs
1	whole egg, beaten
4	cups vegetable oil for deep frying

Place cooked sticky rice into a mixing bowl. Add salt, cheese, Thai seasoning, cilantro and egg. Mix thoroughly and set aside.

Prepare stuffing. Place all ingredients except breadcrumbs and egg in a bowl and mix them thoroughly. Sprinkle some breadcrumbs on the palm of your hand, scoop a generous amount of prepared rice and flatten on your palm. Place $1^{1}/_{2}$ to 2 tablespoons of stuffing in the middle of the rice. Place small amount of rice on top of stuffing and slowly close your hand. Sprinkle small amount of breadcrumbs on top and start to mold rice into a ball. Keep adding breadcrumbs until the ball no longer sticks to your hand and rice ball is firm.

Dip breadcrumb-coated rice ball into beaten egg, remove quickly and coat it again with more breadcrumbs. Squeeze the coated rice ball gently while adding more breadcrumbs and set aside. Repeat until finished.

Place oil into a medium deep saucepan over low heat. Slowly place 3 balls into the saucepan and keep rotating rice balls until they turn golden brown (about 2-3 minutes) Transfer cooked rice balls to paper towels and keep repeating until finished. To make it crispier, place cooked rice ball into a preheated oven at 400° and bake for 10 to 12 minutes.

This rice ball can be eaten hot or cold and it doesn't need any sauce. If you'd like a sauce, turn to other recipes in this book for a sauce that you may like. Personally I like it without the sauce; it stands on its own.

Have a ball! ❖

Prosciutto Pot Stickers

The most expensive ingredient in this recipe is prosciutto, and if you cannot find it in your local market, you can substitute with Canadian bacon or smoked ham. But prosciutto, especially from Parma Italy, is worth it.

❖ *Recipe for 4 to 6*

- $1\frac{1}{2}$ cups all purpose flour
- $\frac{1}{2}$ cup sweet or sticky rice flour
- $\frac{3}{4}$ cup warm water
- $\frac{1}{4}$ teaspoon sea salt
- $\frac{3}{4}$ cup all purpose flour for kneading

Filling

- 2 cups boiling water
- 2 cups shredded radicchio
- 1 cup finely diced prosciutto
- $1\frac{1}{2}$ cups finely shredded Asiago cheese
- 2 tablespoons finely chopped Italian parsley
- 2 teaspoons black pepper cracked
- 3 tablespoons olive oil to pan fry pot stickers
- $\frac{2}{3}$ cup cold water to steam pot stickers

Sauce

- $\frac{1}{3}$ cup balsamic vinegar
- 2 tablespoons sweet black bean sauce or sweet soy sauce (Thai style)
- 1 teaspoon honey
- 2 teaspoons finely minced Italian parsley
- 1 tablespoon Crispy pan roasted garlic (see page 192 for instructions)

Combine all-purpose and sticky rice flour in a stainless steel mixing bowl. Stir with a wooden spoon to allow flour to mix thoroughly. Create a well in the middle of the bowl. Dissolve salt warm water and pour directly into the well. With a wooden spoon, stir the mixture together until stiff and the dough begins to pull away from the bowl. Transfer the dough onto a lightly floured surface. You can knead with the heels of your hands or with your fingers by pushing away from you and then fold the dough towards you while kneading, and rotate the dough a quarter turn clockwise. Knead for 4 to 5 minutes or until the dough turns smooth. Transfer the dough back into the mixing bowl and cover with a dampened cloth and let the dough rest for 45 minutes to an hour.

Meanwhile, blanch radicchio in boiling water for a minute, drain and rinse with cold water. Squeeze the excess water out and place into a mixing bowl. Add prosciutto, cheese, parsley and black pepper. Combine ingredients thoroughly and set aside.

Remove the dough to a lightly floured surface and knead for another 3-4 minutes and roll the dough into a 10-inch long log. Divide log into 20 pieces with a sharp knife or metal dough scraper. Roll each one into a ball and cover with dampened cloth. Flatten each ball with your fingers and using a floured rolling pin, roll the ball into $3\frac{3}{4}$- 4 inch round, dust with flour and set aside. Keep repeating until finished. Hold a round of flattened dough in one hand and place the stuffing into the middle of the dough. Use water to moisten around the edges and fold the dough into a half moon shape and pinch the edges to seal.

Place the stuffed dough onto a lightly floured sheet pan and repeat with the remaining dough. Place 1-$^1/_2$ tablespoons of olive oil in a nonstick skillet over medium heat. Arrange half the Prosciutto pot stickers flat side down into the pan and cook for 1$^1/_2$ to 2 minutes or until the bottom turns golden brown. Add $^1/_3$ cup water, cover tightly with a lid and cook for 3-4 minutes or until water is totally evaporated. Repeat with the remaining pot stickers. Remove and serve right away.

* **F**or dipping sauce, place balsamic vinegar and sweet black bean sauce into a small sauce pan over medium low heat and bring the mixture to a boil. Reduce heat to low. Add honey and simmer for ten minutes. Remove sauce to small sauce cup and let it cool completely before adding remaining ingredients. ❖

Shrimp in the Blanket with Sweet Plum Sauce

You may call this dish Thai Stick, but I don't want people to mistake it for something else that has the same name. I think naming this dish Shrimp in the Blanket makes sense even though they are wrapped in a spring roll sheet and not a blanket. I like tasty food and the marinade makes the shrimp tastier, instead of plain old shrimp. The coconut and sesame seeds lift the flavors up to another level. You may serve this dish just the way it is or you can serve it with the sweet plum sauce.

❖ *Recipe serves 6 to 8*

$^1/_2$	pack spring roll sheets
Marinade	
24	shrimp shelled, deveined and tail intact (about a pound)
$^1/_2$	tablespoon Thai fish sauce seasoning
1	tablespoon light soy sauce
1	tablespoon roasted sesame oil
1	tablespoon salt-free Thai seasoning
1	teaspoon ground white pepper
1	cup toasted shredded coconut
1$^1/_2$	tablespoons toasted white sesame seeds
3	cups vegetable oil for deep frying

Food glue	
1	tablespoon tapioca flour or corn starch
$^1/_4$	cup cold water
Sweet plum sauce	
$^1/_2$	cup water
$^1/_2$	cup sugar
$^1/_4$	cup rice vinegar
$^1/_4$	cup plum sauce
1	teaspoon sea salt
2	tablespoons ground roasted peanuts (salt free)
1	tablespoon finely minced flat leaf parsley or cilantro leaves
1	whole pineapple peeled and sliced into rings

Recipe continue next page ▸

Place shrimp and marinade ingredients into a large mixing bowl. Coat shrimp thoroughly and set aside for 15 minutes.

Combine tapioca flour and water in a small saucepan over low heat, stirring constantly to prevent the mixture from becoming lumpy. When the mixture gets thick like glue, about 1 to 1-$^{1}/_{2}$ minutes, it is ready to be used. Remove this food glue to a small bowl and let it cool before using.

Place one marinated shrimp on a spring roll sheet; sprinkle coconut and sesame seeds around the sheet. With both hands, hold one end of the spring roll sheet to cover shrimp, hold firm and start to roll. Dip a finger into the food glue and spread it on the end of the sheet, then continue rolling to completely enclose the shrimp. The marinated shrimp is trapped inside the spring roll sheet like a blanket. Repeat with remaining shrimp and sheets.

Place sauce ingredients except peanuts and parsley into a small skillet over high heat and bring to a boil. Reduce heat to low and simmer for 5 to 6 minutes or until sauce becomes syrupy. Remove sauce to a bowl and let it completely cool before adding remaining ingredients.

While sauce is cooling, heat vegetable oil in a medium deep skillet over medium heat (about 300°F to 325°F). Deep fry Shrimp in Blankets, 8 to 9 at a time and cook for 2 to 3 minutes until browned on all sides. Remove and drain on paper towels. Repeat with remaining shrimp. Serve hot or at room temperature. ❖

Spring roll sheets have 25 sheets in a package. You can buy them at any Asian market or supermarket chain that knows the current trends in the food world. The market may stock them in either the refrigerator or frozen food section. For this recipe you need to fold and cut them in half. If you can't find the spring roll sheet, you may substitute with rice sheet (the same sheet use in Summer Roll recipe) or wonton skin. The wonton will make this dish a slightly different flavor. When you entertain a large group of friends and you prefer them to mingle around, this is a great dish to serve passed on a tray.

Sugarcane Shrimp

Thailand grows a lot of sugarcane, especially in Kanchana Buri Province. The city of Kanchana Buri is located next to the River Kwai. Also this is where the infamous Bridge Over River Kwai is located. We had a chance to tape one of my TV segments about this railroad story where many human lives were lost unnecessarily. You'd think we humans would have learned. It is said for every mile of railway, there was three hundred ninety lives lost. The railway was known as the death railway. Today you can visit and take the scenic train ride along the River Kwai. When you make this recipe and just before you devour this sweet savory shrimp, please pause for a moment in respect for the lost souls.

❖ *Recipe serves 6 to 8*

Stuffing
1 lb. fresh shrimp shelled and deveined
1 teaspoon sea salt
1 tablespoon roasted sesame oil
2 teaspoons ground white pepper
2 tablespoons finely minced parsley or cilantro
2 tablespoons tapioca flour

Sugarcane stick
18* Sugarcane cut into $^{1}/_{4}$ by 5 to 6 inches in length
$^{1}/_{2}$ cup all purpose flour
2 cups vegetable oil for deep frying
$^{1}/_{4}$ cup seracha chili pepper sauce

Combine shrimp ingredients in a food processor and chop until smooth, scrape shrimp mixture into a bowl. Place a small amount of stuffing mixture on one side of the sugar cane stick and press gently to form 2 inches of stuffing that wraps around the sugar cane. Repeat until finished.

Place stuffed sugar cane stick into a steamer and steam for 5 minutes and transfer to paper towel to remove excess water.

Place oil into a small deep skillet over medium heat. Add steamed sugarcane shrimp and fry for 2 to 3 minutes. Remove fried sugarcane shrimp stick to a paper towel to remove excess oil and transfer to a serving plate. You can serve Sugarcane Shrimp by itself or with a Thai Seracha chili pepper sauce.

* Sugarcane is also packed in a can and you can purchase in most Asian markets. ❖

● The Bridge over the River Kwai.

Summer Rolls with Mango Yogurt Mint Sauce

This dish originated in Vietnam but the stuffing is my style. The original sauce is made of white vinegar, fish sauce, sugar and thinly shredded string carrots. I created a new sauce to make it more tasty and refreshing. This is a great summer dish, very light and easy to make and you don't use too much heat in the kitchen!. Today it's very hot in my garage where I'm writing this recipe. I've lost at least a pound or two and I'm so hot that I had to go outside and hose down my roof to cool it off. I think I'm going to make this for my kids' dinner tonight.

❖ *Recipes serves 4 to 6*

Stuffing

- 8 sheets rice paper
- 6 oz. soft Mee Krob noodles (see page 194 for instructions)
- $1\frac{1}{2}$ cups fresh bean sprouts
- 8 sprigs cilantro
- 32 leaves fresh mint or basil
- 1 cup finely shredded carrot (2-3 inches in length)
- 1 cup shredded green mango (2-3 inches in length)
- 2 cups mixed baby vegetables
- $1\frac{1}{2}$ cups cooked crab or lobster
- 6 cups lukewarm water in deep sheet pan or large bowl
- 4 tablespoons cornstarch glue (see Shrimp in the Blanket recipe page 36 for instructions)

Sauce

- $\frac{1}{4}$ cup coconut milk
- $\frac{1}{2}$ cup low fat yogurt or sour cream
- $\frac{1}{2}$ teaspoon salt
- 1 tablespoon palm sugar or honey
- 12 leaves fresh mint
- 1 cup ripe mango chunks
- 9 Dampened cloth napkins

Combine sauce ingredients in a blender and blend until sauce becomes smooth. Place sauce in a plastic squeeze bottle and paint sauce in any design on a large platter.

Dip one sheet of rice paper into the water, quickly remove and place on one cloth napkin. Place another dampened napkin over the rice sheet. Repeat until finished.

Place $\frac{1}{8}$ of the stuffing ingredients in a strip diagonally across the sheet, just off center, leaving a 2-inch margin at each end. Fold up smaller half of rice sheet to cover stuffing and roll once. Fold in left and right sides to cover stuffing. Spread larger half at the edge of rice sheet with cornstarch glue and continue rolling to completely enclose stuffing, pressing to seal. Slice each finished summer roll into six pieces, and arrange around the platter. ❖

Thai Pot Stickers

You can make your own pot sticker dough and have great fun with it if you try. But it's all right if you chicken out. You may opt to buy it at any Asian or well-stocked supermarket. Substitute with 20 dumpling skins or thick won ton skins

❖ *Recipe serves 4*

- 1 cup all purpose flour
- $^{1}/_{2}$ cup sticky rice flour
- $^{3}/_{4}$ cup all purpose flour for kneading
- $^{3}/_{4}$ cup hot water

Filling

- $^{3}/_{4}$ cup finely minced or ground shrimp
- $^{3}/_{4}$ cup finely minced or ground chicken breast
- $1^{1}/_{2}$ cups finely shredded cabbage
- 3 tablespoons finely minced, peeled fresh ginger
- $^{1}/_{2}$ cup finely sliced scallions
- 1 tablespoon sesame oil
- 1 cup finely chopped apple or jicama
- 2 tablespoons cilantro leaves finely chopped
- 1 teaspoon salt-free Thai seasoning (see glossary page 205)
- 1 tablespoon granulated garlic
- 1 teaspoon white pepper
- 1 tablespoon Thai light soy sauce
- 1 tablespoon Thai fish sauce seasoning
- 3 tablespoon olive oil for pan frying
- $^{2}/_{3}$ cup fresh water for steaming

Sauce

- 2 tablespoons light soy sauce
- $^{1}/_{2}$ cup Rice vinegar
- 2 tablespoons finely minced, peeled fresh ginger
- 2 tablespoons finely minced Italian parsley
- 2 tablespoons finely diced scallions

Combine all-purpose and sticky rice flour in a stainless or glass mixing bowl. Stir with a wooden spoon to allow flour to mix thoroughly, and create a well in the middle of the bowl. Dissolve salt in warm water and pour directly into the well, stir the mixture with a wooden spoon until stiff, and the dough begins to pull away from the bowl.Transfer the dough onto a lightly floured surface. You can knead with the heels of your hands or with your fingers by pushing away from you and then folding the dough towards you while kneading. Rotate the dough occasionally, a quarter turn clockwise. Knead for 4 to 5 minutes or until the dough turns smooth. Transfer the dough back into the mixing bowl and cover with a dampened cloth and let the dough rest for 45 minutes to an hour. Meanwhile place filling ingredients into a bowl and mix them thoroughly.

Remove the dough to a lightly floured surface and knead for another 3-4 minutes and roll the dough into a 10-inch long log. Divide log into 20 pieces with a sharp knife or metal dough scraper. Roll each one into a ball and cover with dampened cloth. Flatten each ball with your fingers and using a floured rolling pin, roll the ball into $3^{3}/_{4}$-4 inch rounds, dust with flour and set aside. Keep repeating until you finish. Hold round flattened dough in one hand and place the stuffing into the middle of the dough. Use water to moisten around the edges and fold the dough into a half moon shape and pinch the edges to seal. Place the stuffed dough on a lightly floured baking sheet and repeat with the remaining dough.

Place $1^1/_2$ tablespoons of olive oil into a nonstick skillet over medium heat. Arrange stuffed dough flat side down in the pan and cook for 1 minute or until the bottom turns golden brown. Add $^1/_3$ cup water, cover tightly with a lid, and cook for 3-4 minutes or until water is totally evaporated. Remove and serve right away.

For dipping sauce, mix ingredients in a sauce bowl. ❖

● "Temple of Dawn" of Thailand's third capital across the Chao Praya River from Bangkok.

● The Anceint capital Sukhothai.

My Favorite Place - Chiang Mai

After watching Tommy Tang's demo tapes back in 1993, I thought to myself "Who is this guy?" Coming from a seasoned public television background of many years I never saw a character quite like Tommy. That same year I finally met Tommy, and again I thought to myself, "Who is this guy?" He was talking about cooking, not just the basics, but how flavors from different cultures can work together. When I saw Tommy teaching a cooking class, I began daydreaming of what Thailand must be like... exotic, tropical, different cultures and of course the fabulous food that he was demonstrating. After his class, I realized this guy was for real ... a teacher, an entertainer — flamboyant, cutting edge, fusion, and a knowledgeable chef. So, after a year of fundraising, TOMMY TANG'S MODERN THAI CUISINE, the TV show, became a reality and we went off to Thailand on Thanksgiving Day 1994.

Well, now as the semi-seasoned traveler of six adventures to Thailand with Tommy, I must admit that my favorite destination is the City of Chiang Mai and environs located in northern Thailand. Chiang Mai is my favorite location not just because of the great people and friends, the hilltribes, the night bazaar, crafts, or food (make sure to visit "The Come In House" Kuhn Nit's restaurant). But because of a very special place, Doi Suthep, a beautiful, serene, peaceful and a holy temple located just outside of Chiang Mai. As you drive up the mountain to the temple the air gets cooler (from 90 to 80) and fresher. Sometimes you will not see anything because of the mist but other times you will have a beautiful panorama of the city of Chiang Mai and the surrounding valley. But still, that's not the reason; Doi Suthep gives one peace of mind and a reflection of life. And, oh yes, if you walk up the final dragon steps to the temple it's a great workout, so don't take the tram. The temple is so magical and historical. To all Buddhists it's a very powerful pilgrimage and even to others it is still an incredible place of beauty and wonder. The locals say that if you don't visit Doi Suthep when in Chiang Mai you haven't visited the North at all. So then, every time I have been to Thailand, I have always visited my favorite location, Doi Suthep and Chiang Mai, whether I'm working or not.

Tom Merklinger

Carrot Salad

When I came to the States 29 years ago and tried American carrot salad, the kind with raisins, it was a bit too sweet for my taste. I had fun making my own version and I think it turned out great. So try it, it's easy to make and is good for you and if you want to put raisins in it, go right ahead. I like to eat this with steamed sticky rice.

❖ *Recipe serves 4*

- 6 whole Kee Noo chilies or 3 Serrano chilies
- 2 cloves fresh garlic
- $^1/_4$ cup small dried shrimp or cooked shrimp cut into small pieces
- $^1/_4$ cup whole roasted unsalted peanuts
- 2 tablespoons palm sugar
- 1 cup string beans or Thai long beans
- 4 cups shredded carrot
- 1 cup diced tomatoes or cherry tomatoes
- 3 tablespoons Thai fish sauce seasoning
- 5 tablespoons lime juice
- A variety of lettuce leaves or half a cabbage

Pound chilies and garlic in a mortar with a pestle for a minute. Add dried shrimp, peanuts, palm sugar and crush ingredients to small pieces. Add string beans and carrots, and pound until soft. Add tomatoes and pound for a minute. Add fish sauce and lime juice and toss ingredients until thoroughly mixed. Transfer carrot salad to a serving plate and serve with lettuce leaves and cabbage. ❖

● Barley field, Chiang Rai.

Grilled Thai Eggplant with Kaffir Lime Sauce

When you ask for Thai eggplant in a Thai or other Asian market, be prepared to answer, what kind of Thai eggplant? Thais have many varieties of eggplant with different colors and shapes, long, round or egg shape, purple, green and white. Some are tiny as grapes and of course I call them grape eggplant. It looks like a cluster of grapes. In this recipe I use either green or purple long eggplant. I particularly like the long green variety, it tastes sweeter. If you are confused just look at the photo on page 198 of this book.

❖ *Recipe Serves 4*

- 4 long Thai eggplants (purple or green)
- 1 tablespoon chopped garlic
- 2 whole crushed Kee Noo chilies
- 1/2 tablespoon palm sugar
- 2 tablespoons Thai fish sauce
- 3 tablespoons lime or lemon juice
- 2 tablespoons thinly sliced lemongrass, tender part only
- 2 tablespoons thinly sliced Kaffir lime leaves

Grill eggplants on a pre-heated grill. If you don't have a grill, substitute with a wire rack over medium heat on a gas burner and grill until they are blistered. Remove blistered skin, cut eggplants into one-inch cubes and arrange inside a round mold on serving plates. Remove the mold carefully.

In a mixing bowl combine garlic, Kee Noo chili, palm sugar, fish sauce and lime juice. Whisk until palm sugar is melted. Pour mixture over eggplant and sprinkle with lemongrass and Kaffir lime leaves.❖

● **Don Whuy Temple Market near The Rose Garden Aprime Resort.**

Grilled Portabella Mushrooms with Balsamic Dill Vinaigrette

I *love this meaty mushroom. This is a good substitute for beef, especially when I long for red meat. You feel like you are eating a piece of meat, it can fill you up for hours and you don't feel stuffed. You can even use one of these grilled mushrooms on a bun in place of a burger. Use this simple vinaigrette with other vegetables, too. It is wonderful for basting any vegetable while you are grilling or searing them.*

❖ *Recipe serves 4*

- 2 large portabella mushrooms
- 3 tablespoons olive oil
- 1 tablespoon salt-free Thai seasoning
- 1 whole red bell pepper
- 1 bunch frise lettuce, rinsed and drained
- 4 cloves thinly sliced garlic (for topping)
- 2 tablespoons virgin olive oil for sautéing garlic slices

Vinaigrette

- 3 tablespoons Thai light soy sauce
- 4 tablespoons balsamic vinegar
- 1 teaspoon honey or sugar
- 4 tablespoons fresh dill

Place half the olive oil into a small skillet over medium low heat. Add garlic and stir constantly for $2\frac{1}{2}$ to 3 minutes or until garlic turns golden brown. Remove garlic to paper towel and save oil for dressing.

Roast bell pepper on a wire rack over a low heat gas burner flame or grill until blistered on all sides, turning frequently. Transfer blistered bell pepper to a small paper or plastic bag, close bag and let the pepper cool. Peel and seed bell pepper, slice into small strips and set aside.

Thoroughly coat mushrooms with olive oil and Thai seasoning. Place mushrooms on the grill or into a sauté pan over medium heat and grill or sear for 3 to 4 minutes on each side. Transfer cooked mushrooms to a cutting board and cut into 8 to 10 slices.

Combine vinaigrette ingredients in a large mixing bowl. Add reserved garlic olive oil and whisk to blend. Add frise lettuce and toss until coated. Transfer to serving plates. Arrange portabella mushroom around lettuce. Add roasted bell pepper on top and sprinkle with crispy garlic. ❖

Heart of Romaine Salad with Sesame Ginger Soy Vinaigrette

This salad is so easy to make and so tasty. If you don't want to hassle with tomatoes that's okay too. I think this simple arrangement makes the salad more appealing to your guests. And you really feel that you made a beautiful plate.

❖ *Recipe serves 4*

4 hearts of romaine lettuces
4 medium tomatoes
16 yellow cherry tomatoes cut in half

Vinaigrette

2 tablespoons roasted sesame oil
2 tablespoons light soy sauce
3 tablespoons rice vinegar
1 tablespoon finely grated fresh ginger
2 teaspoons finely chopped fresh garlic
$^1/_2$ teaspoon sea salt
1 teaspoon cracked black pepper
1 teaspoon honey

Cut about $^1/_3$ to $^1/_2$ inch off the top and bottom of the tomatoes. With a small paring knife, remove the inside pulp but make sure not to puncture the tomato shell.

Insert heart of romaine lettuce into the tomatoes, gently push it until it is tight and slice off the ends of the romaine if they are too tall. Place tomatoes standing up on the serving plate.

Put sauce ingredients into a plastic squeeze bottle and shake it vigorously until blended. Squeeze vinaigrette over romaine and garnish with yellow cherry tomatoes around the serving plates. ❖

● Fruit and vegetable carvings.

Tree of Life Salad with Fat-Free Lemongrass Vinaigrette

When I created this fat-free vinaigrette recipe my customers in the restaurant questioned the fat content because they couldn't believe that without oil it can taste this good. So I had to show them how we made it and still, they didn't believe it. Well, you can't always win. The secret is palm sugar.

So please give it a try.

❖ *Recipe serves 4*

- 5 cups mixed baby lettuces (arugula, radicchio, frise, red-leaved lettuce, romaine) 5-6 oz.
- 4 medium tomatoes
- 20 thin long strips of red bell pepper $3^1/_2$- 4 inches
- 20 thin long strips of yellow bell pepper $3^1/_2$- 4 inches
- 20 thin long strips of carrots $3^1/_2$- 4 inches
- 50 long strand crispy silver noodles
- 2 tablespoons finely diced red bell pepper
- 2 tablespoons finely diced yellow bell pepper
- 2 tablespoons finely diced carrots

Vinaigrette

- 2 tablespoons Thai fish sauce seasoning
- 1 tablespoon lime or lemon juice
- 2 tablespoons rice vinegar
- 1 teaspoon finely chopped Kee Noo chili
- 2 teaspoons finely chopped garlic
- 1 teaspoon palm sugar or honey
- 2 tablespoons very finely diced lemongrass

Slice top and bottom off tomatoes, core and remove pulp. Arrange mixed baby lettuces to create a bouquet and stuff into the tomatoes. Trim the excess off the lettuce. Place the lettuce bouquet on a plate. Arrange strips of red and yellow bell pepper, carrot and crispy noodles around the lettuce.

Place sauce ingredients into a plastic bottle and shake until thoroughly mixed, water the tree of life with vinaigrette and fertilize the tree with diced bell peppers and carrots. ❖

Puk Boong Salad with Tamarind Vinaigrette

If you like spinach or watercress, you'll love this salad. Thais love this vegetable so much that they eat it at least 4 times a week. I like it because when I was young someone told me that if you eat Puk Boong every day you would be smart. Yeah right; but I love it anyway.

❖ *Recipe serves 4*

- 12 cups Puk Boong rinsed in cold water
- 3 cups water
- 1 7 to 8 ounce skinless and boneless chicken breast
- 2 tablespoons roasted garlic
- 1/2 cup sliced crispy shallots
- 1/4 cup ground roasted unsalted peanuts

Vinaigrette

- 1 tablespoon roasted chili paste
- 2 tablespoons palm sugar or honey
- 3 tablespoons Thai fish sauce seasoning
- 1 teaspoon finely chopped garlic
- 1/4 cup tamarind juice (See page 197 for instructions)
- 1 tablespoon rice vinegar
- 1/2 teaspoon dried Kee Noo chili flakes
- 1/4 cup coconut milk

Rinse Puk Boong in cold water, drain and set aside. Bring water to a boil in a small pan over medium heat. Add chicken breast and boil for 15 minutes. Turn off the heat, remove chicken from water, let it cool and tear into small strips and set aside.

Place coconut milk into a small saucepan over medium heat and bring to a boil. Remove and let it cool.

Combine vinaigrette ingredients, including coconut milk, in a mixing bowl and whisk until blended. Add Puk Boong and chicken strips, toss thoroughly and transfer to serving plates. Sprinkle crispy garlic, crispy shallots and peanuts on top and serve. ❖

Puk Boong is a Thai vegetable whose flavor is hard to describe. The closest vegetables that I can compare it to are spinach and watercress. The flavor is much milder and tastier, but you'll have to try it and find out for yourself. I call it water spinach, and the reason is because it grows best in water, especially rivers or canals. I'd like you to call it by the right name, what else, Puk Boong! So when you visit Thailand make sure to order it. You can eat it fresh in salads or sauté it with garlic, Kee Noo chili, fermented soybeans and sweet black bean sauce. I could eat this every day, and it goes well with Kai Kra Prao.

Someone told me that during World War 2, prisoners at the Bridge over the River Kwai prison camp escaped the Japanese by jumping into the river at night and hiding under a massive stand of Puk Boong that grew on the river. They used the Puk Boong stem as a straw to breathe under the water. I actually tried it and it worked.

● Vegetation on Chiang Mai hill.

Floating Market

SOUP

Whenever I visit Thailand, either with my family for vacation or taping my TV series, I love to visit the Floating Market. There used to be many floating markets around Bangkok, but polluted waters in the canals and streets replacing waterways has forced this charming way of life to all but disappear.

Nowadays, when we would like to visit one, we have to go to Dam-Noen-Sa-Duak, Ratchaburi province, which remains one of the busiest floating markets around.This market is quite a trek if you stay in a Bangkok hotel. Instead, we love to stay at the Rose Garden Aprime Resort, which is located 20 miles outside of Bangkok. This resort is our favorite place to stay.

When you enter the resort, you feel like you're entering the "Secret Garden", nothing outside matters here. I love to walk around and smell the flowers, especially the roses, after all this is the Rose Garden! At night, we enjoy having dinner at a Thai restaurant next to the river, and then taste some Thai wines at the boathouse. The resort is so quiet and dark at night you can see the fireflies chasing each other. (When was the last time you saw a firefly?)

In the morning, you have a chance to do a good deed, by offering food to the monks, who paddle the small canoes. Now it's time to leave for the Floating Market. When you arrive at the market, you will see the merchants paddling from small to larger boats, selling their freshly picked fruits, vegetables and flowers. There are many kinds of foods, and spices and other household goods for daily needs. You can rent a canoe and be part of the locomotion and feel what it is like to maneuver the boat around the canal traffic. When there are too many boats it creates a water traffic jam! Each boat courteously allows the others to pass by, but sometimes you can hear an argument when someone is being selfish. After seeing so many foods on the boats, it makes you hungry, oh well! Order some food, yes, that's right! You can buy anything here including a plate of Pad Thai noodles and Thai iced coffee.

On the way back we'll stop by the largest Golden Pagoda in Nakorn Pathom, to pay our respects before returning to the resort for an afternoon dip in the pool. My daughters, Aisha and Chyna love to swim here; it is an ozone-treated pool, (meaning chemical-free). I prefer to visit a temple market nearby and the Thai cultural village in the resort, and if I'm lucky, there may be a cooking class session there.

Late afternoon, I like to order a sweet fragrant young coconut drink and a plate of Pomelo. Pomelo looks like grapefruit but is much larger and tastes better. This area is also famous for it. I always ask the server to scoop the fresh soft coconut meat and combine it with coconut water and ice, then blend until it becomes slush and pour it back into the coconut shell. Ah! This is heaven.

I once overheard a table discussing their itinerary for visitors from England including the Thai lifestyle, customs, culture and cuisine in the village. It sounded so wonderful; maybe I should do that next time! I'm so relaxed I could easily make the Rose Garden Aprime Resort my second home...

Tommy

Curry Noodles

I am very fond of this noodle. In Bangkok you can find it everywhere. It very spicy and tasty and you know me, I love that tasty. In Thailand we call it Indian Noodles. But when I moved to America, Indian doesn't mean people from India. It can be American Indian. I didn't know that Hindus and Muslims are not getting along. In Thailand, we all live in peace and harmony, no matter what your color or ethnic background. We are all Thai. I didn't know the word "racism" until I moved here. And why do people have to hate each other just because of color of their skin and ethnic origin? I almost named this dish Indian Noodles, but I don't want American Indians to tell me that there is no such dish in their cuisine. And I don't want Muslims to feel hurt by not naming it Muslim Noodles. Why can't we act like a bowl of noodles; it doesn't care who eats them. It's always happy to show off its vibrant colors. It always gives satisfaction for those who seek to taste it. It gives me a happy tasty feeling in my mouth. So! I have chosen the middle path, just like the good book says, and named it Curry Noodles.

❖ *Recipe serves 4 to 6*

- 10 cups water
- 1 can (14 oz.) coconut milk (for stewing)
- $1\frac{1}{2}$ lb. stew beef (beef chuck) cut in to $1\frac{1}{4}$ to $1\frac{1}{2}$ inch cubes
- 2 tablespoons olive oil or vegetable oil
- 2 tablespoons red curry paste
- 1 cup coconut milk (for sauce)
- 1 tablespoon curry powder
- 4 tablespoons Thai fish sauce seasoning
- $1\frac{1}{2}$ tablespoons sugar
- 10 cups water
- 16 oz. soft Pad Thai noodles (see page 194 for instructions)
- 6 oz. fresh bean sprouts
- $\frac{1}{4}$ cup julienne yellow bean curd (tofu)
- 1 tablespoon crispy garlic oil (see page 192 for instructions)
- $\frac{1}{4}$ cup sliced crispy shallots (see page 192 for instructions)
- $\frac{1}{3}$ cup thinly sliced scallions
- 3 tablespoons minced cilantro or parsley
- 4 tablespoons red chili vinegar (see page 190 for instructions)

Combine water, the can of coconut milk and beef into a large stockpot over high heat and bring to a boil. Reduce heat to low, cover with a lid and simmer for $1\frac{1}{2}$ hours or until meat is tender.

Place olive oil and curry paste into a deep skillet over medium heat and sauté for 1 minute. Add $\frac{1}{4}$ cup of coconut milk and stir for 2 minutes. Add remaining 1 cup coconut milk, curry powder, fish sauce, sugar and stir for 2 to 3 minutes. Remove beef from the stock, add to curry sauce and cook for 5 minutes. Transfer beef and curry sauce to beef stock and bring to a boil. Reduce heat to low and simmer for 30 to 45 minutes.

Bring water to a boil in a medium stockpot. Blanch soft Pad Thai noodles and bean sprouts for 1 to $1\frac{1}{2}$ minutes and transfer to a large bowl. Add tofu and crispy garlic olive oil. Transfer beef curry and pour over noodles. Add scallions and cilantro on top. Add red chili vinegar if you prefer. ❖

Chyna Pink Noodles (Yen-Ta-Foe)

This is my daughters Aisha and Chyna's favorite Thai noodle soup, especially Chyna. It must be in the genes and history past. When I was 10 years old, our house was burned down by arson. We had to move to the slums near the Klong-Teoy deep seaport in Bangkok. When my Mom could afford to buy a bowl of this noodle soup, we always asked the vendor to give us extra broth so we could all share. Maybe because I told this story to both my daughters one too many times, it sank into their subconscious. They both loved this soup the first time they tasted it.

❖ *Recipe serves 4*

- 8 cups chicken or vegetable stock (see page 195 for instructions)
- 10 cups boiling water
- 8 oz. soft Mee Krob noodles
- 4 cups Puk Boong (see glossary page 52) substitute with spinach
- 3 oz. thinly sliced pork (optional)
- 8 fish balls
- 8 medium shrimp shelled and deveined
- 2 calamari (baby squid) cleaned and sliced into 1 inch rings
- 1 sheet sliced fried fish cake
- 8 deep-fried soft tofu
- 2 white mushrooms soaked in warm water and cut into small pieces
- 2 tablespoons tomato paste
- 2 teaspoon fermented tofu (optional)
- $1^1/_2$ tablespoons roasted garlic olive oil (see page 194 for instruction)
- $1^1/_2$ tablespoons rice vinegar
- 3 tablespoons Thai fish sauce seasoning
- 1 tablespoon sugar
- 2 tablespoons diced scallions
- 2 tablespoons sliced cilantro leaves
- $^1/_4$ cup fresh ground red chili vinegar optional (see page 190 for instructions)

Bring chicken or vegetable stock to boil in a stockpot over high heat. Add pork and bring to a boil. Reduce heat to low and let it simmer for 15 minutes. Remove pork from the chicken stock and set aside.

Blanch fish balls, shrimp, calamari, fish cake, fried tofu and mushrooms for 1 to 2 minutes in boiling water. Remove to a plate and set aside. Blanch noodles and Puk Boong in the same water for a minute, strain and transfer to a serving bowl. Add tomato paste, garlic oil, rice vinegar, fish sauce and sugar. Arrange blanched seafood, tofu, mushrooms and sliced cooked pork over noodles. Pour chicken stock over noodles, sprinkle with cilantro leaves and scallions. Add red chili vinegar if you prefer it spicier.❖

● **I'm buying grilled bamboo sticky rice.**

Khao-Soi Noodles

***W**hen you have a chance to visit the city of Chiang Mai in the northern part of Thailand, make sure to stop by and try Khao-Soi noodles. It is a must if you ever make it there. The word Khao means rice and the word Soi, I interpret to mean slice. I'm getting confused; how are you going to slice a grain of rice? If you are there in Chiang Mai and happen to find out the meaning of Khao-Soi, please let me know, call me at my restaurant in Los Angeles.*

❖ *Recipe serves 4 to 6*

- $^1/_4$ cup olive oil
- 3 tablespoons curry powder
- $1^1/_2$ tablespoons panang curry paste or red curry paste (see glossary page 205)
- 2 lbs. chicken breast, cut into 1 inch squares
- $2^1/_2$ cups water
- 2 tablespoons palm sugar or regular sugar
- 4 tablespoons Thai fish sauce seasoning

Coconut broth

- 1 can coconut milk
- 3 cups water
- 4 cilantro roots or 8 sprigs, stems and leaves
- $^1/_4$ cup sliced fresh ginger

Noodles

- 10 cups boiling water
- 1 lb. fresh egg noodles, smallest size
- 4 cups fresh bean sprouts
- 2 tablespoons sweet blackbean sauce or sweet soy sauce
- 2 tablespoons lime juice
- $^1/_4$ cup sliced scallions
- $^1/_4$ cup sliced cilantro leaves with stems removed
- 4 to 6 cups crispy egg noodles (see page 193 for instructions)
- $^1/_4$ cup crispy shallot (see page 192 for instructions)
- $^1/_3$ cup diced shallots (optional)
- $^1/_2$ cup pickled sour mustard greens (optional)
- 2 teaspoons chili oil

Place olive oil into a deep skillet over medium heat. Add curry powder and stir for a minute. Add curry paste, turn heat to high and stir for a minute. Add chicken and stir for 2 minutes. Add $^1/_2$ cup water and stir for 3 to 4 minutes. Add palm sugar, fish sauce and remaining water. Stir constantly and bring curry mixture to boil. Reduce heat to medium low and cook for 30 minutes. Remove and set aside. Combine coconut milk, water, cilantro roots and ginger into a large stockpot over high heat and bring boil. Reduce heat to low and simmer for 15 minutes. Coconut broth is ready to be used.

Blanch egg noodles and bean sprouts in boiling water for 1 to $1^1/_2$ minutes, strain and transfer to a large bowl. Add sweet black bean sauce and chicken curry to blanched noodles. Sprinkle with scallions, cilantro, crispy shallots and place crispy noodles on top. ❖

Mama Noodles

Everybody in the world has their own famous Mama chicken noodle soup. I also have one to share with you. I remember when I was young, when I got sick and had a high temperature, my mom would go out to a noodle shop and buy this chicken noodle soup. I would eat every drop of the soup and break out in a sweat. An hour later, I would feel great and be ready to go out and play. Now since she is gone, every time I get sick, I can't help but think of her.

Thanks, Mom, for all those chicken noodle soups. I feel much better now.

❖ *Recipe serves 4*

10	cups water
6	cups chicken stock or vegetable stock (see page 195 for instructions)
$^1/_2$	cup ground chicken breast
16	steamed fish balls
8	sliced fried fish cakes
12	oz. fresh or dried Rad Na noodles (see glossary page 204)
2	cups fresh bean sprouts
1	tablespoon dried preserved cabbage
4	tablespoons Thai fish sauce seasoning
4	teaspoons sugar
4	teaspoons roasted garlic olive oil (sea page 192 for instructions)
4	tablespoons finely sliced scallions
2	tablespoons minced cilantro leaves

Bring chicken stock to a boil in a medium stockpot. Add chicken, steamed fish balls, fish cakes and bring stock to a boil again. Reduce heat to medium and set aside.

Place 10 cups of water in a large stockpot over high heat and bring to boil. Blanch noodles and bean sprouts for 1 to 1$^1/_2$ minutes, drain and transfer to large soup bowl. Add remaining ingredients on top of noodles.

Add boiling chicken stock ingredients into the bowl.

Now feel better! ❖

● **Here is Golden Pagoda Temple, Nakorn Prathom province.**

Meat Ball Noodles

Someone told me that the best Meat Ball noodles shop is in Mae Sai, a city in Chiang Rai Province. The city of Mae Sai is located next to Myanmar, on the border with Thailand, which is also where the famous Golden Triangle is located. If you don't know what the Golden Triangle is, go to the library and find out yourself. It took me three days to get to Mae Sai, because many years ago the road and transportation was not what it is today. What made these noodles special is the chili vinegar that they add to the noodle soup.

Therefore don't leave it out.

❖ *Recipe serves 4*

Stock

- 14 cups water
- $^1/_2$ to 1 lb. chicken bones or beef bones
- 4 cloves garlic, skin intact
- 1 teaspoon whole white peppercorns
- 1 large brown onion cut in half
- 2 sticks celery cut into 4 pieces
- 1 large carrot cut into 4 pieces
- 8 cilantro roots

Meatballs

- 2 cups ground beef, about 1 pound
- $^1/_2$ teaspoon sea salt
- 1 tablespoon tapioca flour
- 1 tablespoon finely minced parsley
- 2 teaspoons granulated garlic
- 1 teaspoon ground white pepper

Noodles

- 8 cups boiling water
- 8 oz. soft Mee Krob or Pad Thai noodles (see page 194 for instructions)
- 1$^1/_2$ tablespoons crispy garlic olive oil (see page 192 for instructions)
- 2 cups fresh bean sprouts
- 4 tablespoons Thai fish sauce seasoning
- 4 teaspoons sugar
- 1 teaspoon ground white pepper
- 2 tablespoons minced cilantro leaves
- $^1/_4$ cup sliced scallions

Chili vinegar

- $^1/_2$ cup thinly sliced Jalapeno chilies
- $^1/_2$ cup rice vinegar

• Me & my TV crew @ The Boarder of Thailand & Myanmar.

Place stock ingredients into a stockpot over high heat and bring to a boil. Reduce heat to low and simmer for 20 to 25 minutes or until reduced by half.

Place meatball ingredients into a food processor and grind until mixed thoroughly and beef becomes a large lumpy ball, then transfer to a bowl. Scoop a generous amount of beef mixture in your hand and roll into a ball $1^1/_4$ to $1^1/_2$ inches round. Continue until finished.

Drop meatballs into the boiling water. Boil for 10 minutes. After they rise to the top of boiling water, remove and set aside to let them cool. The meatballs are now ready to be used for this recipe of noodles soup or for your other favorite dishes.

Blanch soft Mee Krob noodles and bean sprouts in boiling water for a minute and transfer to serving bowls. Add meatballs and remaining ingredients on top of noodles and scoop stock without the herb ingredients and put into the noodles, Garnish with cilantro leaves and spice it up with chili vinegar. ❖

- Santi Buri Golf Course, Chiang Rai province near the Golden Triangle.
- Designed by : Robert Trentjones Jr.

Papa's Duck Noodles

This is my father's favorite noodle soup. Whenever we go out for lunch, I always have to ask him what he would like to eat today. My dad is kind of a quiet guy. He and I hardly talk more than 10 minutes. Maybe because I left home to work and was on my own since I was 11 years old. Now we're much older and much closer than before. I have learned what he likes and dislikes to eat. Today I ordered his favorite noodle soup and I would like to share with you.

❖ *Recipe serves 4*

Duck stock

- 12 cups water
- 4 cilantro roots
- 2 slices ginger
- 4 cloves fresh garlic, skin intact
- 2 sticks cinnamon
- 6 whole cloves
- 3 whole star anise
- 1 teaspoon whole white peppercorns
- 1 teaspoon whole coriander seeds
- 2 tablespoons sweet black bean sauce or sweet soy sauce
- 1/4 cup Thai light soy sauce
- 2 tablespoons Thai fish sauce seasoning
- 2 teaspoons sugar
- 1/2 Long Island duck or Muskovy duck

Noodles

- 8 cups boiling water for blanching
- 8 oz. soft Mee Krob or fresh egg noodles (see page 194 for instructions)
- 2 cups fresh bean sprouts
- 1/4 cup thinly diced scallions
- 2 tablespoons sliced cilantro leaves
- 2 tablespoons crushed red chili vinegar (optional)

Combine stock ingredients, except duck, in a large stockpot over high heat and bring to a boil. Add duck and bring to a boil. Reduce heat to low, cover with a lid and simmer for 1 hour. Remove cooked duck and transfer to cutting board. Remove bones from the duck, thinly slice the meat and set aside. Drain duck stock through a fine sieve into a smaller stockpot. Discard stock herb ingredients. Place stock back on the burner over medium heat.

Bring water to a boil in a stockpot. Blanch noodles and bean sprouts for 1 to 1 1/2 minutes. Drain and transfer to large soup bowl. Arrange sliced duck meat on top of noodles. Add boiling duck stock to noodles. Garnish with scallions and cilantro leaves. ❖

Spicy Basil Noodles

I*t's raining outside. The sky is gray and misty. The cold wind just blew open my window sending a chill up my spine. Yes, it's cold. I need to warm myself up against the wind. Of course soup, but not just any soup. It has to be hot and spicy noodle soup. Lemongrass stock is waiting in the freezer, now let's get started.*

D*ouble for two, triple for three, quadruple for four.*

❖ *Recipe serves 1*

- 2 cups lemongrass stock
- 3 oz. beef, thinly sliced into strips (substitute with chicken or shrimp)
- 3 cups boiling water
- 3 oz. soft Pad Thai noodles (see page 194)
- $1\frac{1}{2}$ cups fresh bean sprouts
- $1\frac{1}{2}$ teaspoons Thai roasted chili paste
- 1 tablespoon Thai fish sauce seasoning
- 2 tablespoons Thai black bean sauce
- $1\frac{1}{2}$ tablespoons lime or lemon juice
- 2 tablespoons ground peanuts
- 1 teaspoon crispy garlic olive oil
- 2 tablespoons sliced scallions
- $1\frac{1}{2}$ tablespoons sliced cilantro leaves
- $\frac{1}{4}$ cup Thai or regular basil leaves
- 1 tablespoon crushed red chili vinegar
- $\frac{1}{2}$ teaspoon dried Kee Noo chili flakes (optional)

Place lemongrass stock into a small stockpot and bring to a boil. Add beef, bring stock to a boil and reduce heat to medium. In another small stockpot bring 3 cups of water to a boil. Add noodles and bean sprouts. Blanch for less than a minute. Remove and drain with colander and place noodles and bean sprouts in a soup bowl. Add remaining ingredients to noodles and pour lemongrass with beef stock into noodles.

Have a warm cold day ❖

● Offering food to the monks.

Home Made Beef Stew Noodles

When I wanted to have a meaty noodle soup, I would order this soup from the noodle shop in Bangkok. I later moved to the U.S. and found out that in Los Angeles, San Francisco and New York, Chinatown has it too. This soup is great for a cold winter day. It takes a long time to cook, so don't just cook for yourself. Invite your family and friends. I made this soup while writing this book in Angola, near Buffalo City, New York. I made this soup and of course I invited Al, Sr., and Joyce Ruggiero and all their families and friends to join me. I made enough for the army.

❖ *Recipe serves 8*

Beef stock

- 2 lbs. pre-cut stew beef
- 1 tablespoon olive oil
- 24 cups water
- 4 sticks cinnamon $3^1/_2$ to 4 inch lengths
- 1 large brown onion cut into half with skin on
- 6 pieces dried galanga, sliced
- 6 whole fresh or dried kaffir lime leaves (substitute with bay leaves)
- 10 cloves large garlic, cracked with skin on
- 2 teaspoons whole black peppercorns
- 1 teaspoon whole coriander seeds
- 6 roots cilantro or whole sprigs (substitute with Italian parsley)
- $^1/_2$ cup Thai light soy sauce
- 2 tablespoons rice vinegar or vegetable vinegar
- $^1/_2$ cup Thai sweet black bean sauce
- $^1/_3$ cup Thai fish sauce seasoning
- 24 whole white-cap mushrooms

Noodles

- 8 oz. fresh bean sprouts
- 1 lb. soft Mee krob noodles
- 1 cup sliced scallions
- 1 cup sliced cilantro or parsley leaves
- $^1/_2$ cup crispy shallots (see page 192)
- $^1/_4$ cup crispy garlic and oil (see page 192)
- $^1/_3$ cup red chili vinegar (see page 190) (optional)
- 2 tablespoons dried Kee Noo chili flakes (optional)
- 2 teaspoons ground white pepper

Placc stew beef and olive oil into a large skillet over high heat and sear until beef is charred on all sides (about 4 to 5 minutes). Remove and set aside.

Bring water to a boil in a large stockpot. Add all beef stock ingredients except mushrooms and bring to a boil. Reduce heat to medium low and cover with a lid and simmer for one hour. Add mushrooms and keep simmering for another hour. Beef stew is ready to be used.

Blanched soft Mee Krob noodles and bean sprouts in boiling water for 1 to $1^1/_2$ minutes. Drain and put equal amounts into 8 large soup bowls. Add scallions, cilantro, crispy shallots and crispy garlic to 8 bowls. Place beef stew over noodles, sprinkle with white pepper and serve with crushed red chili vinegar and chili flakes. ❖

Tami Boat Noodles

My friend Tami, from Houston, went to Thailand with my family and me. She has been to Thailand with us many times. On the Thai Airways flight she kept asking me to make sure we would stop by the Floating Market so she could have her favorite Boat Noodles soup. I said yes, yes and yes. We did stop by the Floating Market one day but her heart was so broken. The canoe that sells Boat Noodles was not there. I later found out that the boat lady was sick that day. Here it is Tami; this recipe is for you.

❖ *Recipe serves 4*

Stock

- 14 cups water
- 4 pieces dried galangal
- 4 cloves garlic, skin intact
- 2 sticks cinnamon, 3 to 4 inches long
- 1 teaspoon whole white peppercorns
- 1 large brown onion cut in half
- 2 sticks celery cut into 4 pieces
- 1 large carrot cut into 4 pieces
- 8 cilantro roots
- 2 tablespoons sweet black bean sauce
- $1\frac{1}{2}$ cups chuck beef cut into $1\frac{1}{2}$ inches cube

Noodles ingredients

- 16 Thai-style meat balls
- 8 cups boiling water
- 8 oz. soft Mee Krob or Pad Thai noodles (see page 194 for instructions)
- 4 cups Puk-Boong or spinach (see photo on page 198)
- 2 cups fresh bean sprouts
- $1\frac{1}{2}$ tablespoons crispy garlic olive oil (see page 192 for instructions)
- 4 tablespoons Thai fish sauce seasoning
- 4 teaspoons sugar
- 1 teaspoon ground white pepper
- 2 tablespoons minced cilantro leaves
- $\frac{1}{4}$ cup sliced scallions
- 1 cup pork rind pieces (optional)
- 2 tablespoons red chili vinegar (see page 190 for instructions) (optional)
- 2 teaspoons Kee-Noo chili flakes (optional)

Place stock ingredients into a large stockpot over high heat and bring to a boil. Reduce heat to medium and cook for 20 minutes. Add meat balls, reduce heat to low and simmer for 20 minutes. Skim and discard fat that floats to the top of stock. Stock is ready to be used for Boat Noodles.

Place water into a medium stockpot over high heat and bring to a boil. Blanch soft noodles, Puk Boong and bean sprouts for 1 to $1\frac{1}{2}$ minutes and drain in a strainer to remove excess water. Transfer to large soup bowl or four separate soup bowls.

Remove beef and meatballs from beef stock and put on top of blanched noodles. Add remaining ingredients and carefully ladle beef stock without the herb ingredients and pour into the noodles. Sprinkle with cilantro leaves, scallions and pork rind and spice it up with chili vinegar. ❖

Life on the canal, or klong, as we Thais call it, seems very harsh and hectic to visitors. But for most people who live day-by-day, making ends meet on the canal can be a peaceful living in harmony with nature.

Many people feel it would be helpful to change the way the canal dwellers live, to create a better standard of living for them. But are we to make such an assumption for them? Just because we mean well, does not mean we should give them a cement-paved road over their klong so they can travel more efficiently. We would be changing something that is uniquely Thai, and destroying their travel by boat and paddling by canoe, that is their heritage and harmonious tradition. Instead, we should just educate the canal dwellers of the importance of non-pollution, and find better ways to clean and maintain the klongs, and build more sewage treatment plant, so that household water can be channeled through the cleaning plant before returning to the Gulf of Siam.

I, who was born in Bangkok, have seen so many changes in the canal way of living. When I was young, many years ago, I used to swim in a canal called klong Sa-Thon. It was lined with trees and a small road. I used to pick green mangos from the trees and eat them without peeling the skin because we didn't use pesticides in those days. The tart flavor of young mango and its sour taste gave satisfaction to the hungry kids. Now for the sake of development, transportation, and a "better" way of life, this klong is now paved with cement and that is what is happening to klongs throughout Thailand.

I'm back in Bangkok once again, standing on the street, looking at the same klong where I used to swim. I look at the end of the canal, and remember when we raced each other to see who reached the Chao Praya River first. The canal ended at the river. But I no longer see the end of the klong; instead, I see a huge bridge crossing over the river. The new generation won't have a chance to know what life was be like, tasting the green mango from the trees lining the klong called Sa-Thon.

Tommy

Lobster Wonton Soup

***I** prefer to make this using whole live lobster or fresh frozen lobster. It makes the wonton stuffing taste better. But if you don't want the hassle of the work you may buy the cooked lobster meat too. I like the fresh lobster because I can use the lobster shell to flavor the stock.*

❖ *Recipe serves 4*

Lobster stock

- 1 whole fresh lobster
- 12 cups water
- 1 whole Spanish onion, skin intact, cut in half
- 1 large carrot cut into small sections
- 2 sticks celery cut into 4 sections
- 4 cilantro roots
- 1 teaspoon sea salt
- 1/2 teaspoon ground white pepper

Won ton filing

- 1 pack wonton wrappers (thin sheet)
- 2 teaspoons roasted virgin sesame oil
- 2 teaspoons granulated garlic
- 1/2 tablespoon light Thai soy sauce
- 1/2 teaspoon ground white pepper
- 1/4 cup water chestnuts finely chopped
- 2 tablespoons cilantro leaves finely sliced — substitute with flat-leaf parsley
- 1 tablespoon chives, finely sliced
- 1 egg white, beaten
- 1/4 cup cold water for sealing wonton wrappers
- 10 cups boiling water
- 1 pack enoki mushrooms
- 1 pack chives for garnish

Remove claws, arms and legs from the lobster. Separate the tail from the head, rinse in cold water thoroughly. Split the tail in half with scissors or a sharp strong knife. Scrape fresh lobster meat from the tail, mince finely and put into a mixing bowl. Add sesame oil, granulated garlic, soy sauce, white pepper, water chestnuts, cilantro, chives and egg white, and mix ingredients thoroughly.

Bring water, onion, carrot, celery and cilantro roots to a boil in a large stockpot over high heat. Reduce heat to medium low and simmer for 20 minutes. Add lobster claws, arms and legs and cook for 6 to 8 to minutes. Remove cooked lobster from the stock and let it cool.

Crack lobster shell with a nutcracker and gently remove the meat. When you crack the lobster claws, try to keep the claw meat in the shell and set aside. Add cleaned lobster head and tail and bring stock to a boil. Reduce heat to low and simmer for 20 minutes. Drain stock in a fine sieve into a medium stockpot. Add sea salt, white pepper and bring stock to a boil. Reduce heat to low and simmer until ready to use.

For lobster wonton, place a small mound of filling mixture in the center of a wonton wrapper. Dip a finger in cold water and wet wonton wrapper around the edge of the skin, fold to close and set aside. Repeat with remaining filling and wrappers. Save leftover wonton wrappers in the freezer.

Bring water to a boil, add prepared lobster wontons and cook for 2 to 3 minutes. When the wontons float to the top, they are done. Remove wontons to 4 soup bowls; add enoki mushrooms, lobster meat and claws. Pour lobster stock over wontons and garnish with chives. ❖

Phuket Noodles

Whenever I go to Phuket Island, I always make a point to find the time to stop by the Phuket noodles shop in downtown Phuket. It is always worth the trek. If you ever make it to this island in the south of Thailand, please, by all means, stop by and have some great noodles, you'll love it. They don't have a store name or I don't remember it. You can call the folks at Phuket Prestige Travel. They can tell you where this noodle shop is located. And while you are in downtown Phuket, you might as well stop by at the cashew nut factory and see how they process cashew nuts.

❖ *Recipe serves 4*

Shrimp stock

- 12 cups boiling water
- 1 whole brown onion cut in half
- 1 large carrot cut into 4 sections
- 2 sticks celery cut into 4 sections
- 4 cilantro roots or 8 springs stems and leaves

Noodles

- 1 tablespoon olive oil
- 8 cups boiling water for blanching
- 4 packs egg noodles (smallest strand)
- 4 oz. fresh bean sprouts
- $^{1}/_{2}$ lb. fresh shrimp, shelled and deveined (save shrimp shells for stock)
- 6 oz. crabmeat
- 8 fish balls
- 8 sliced fried fish cakes
- 4 strips thick bacon (optional)
- 2 tablespoons roasted garlic olive oil (see page 192 for instructions)
- 3 tablespoons Thai fish sauce seasoning
- 1 tablespoon dried preserved cabbage (optional)
- 1 tablespoon sugar
- 4 tablespoons ground roasted salt-free cashew nuts
- $^{1}/_{2}$ teaspoon ground white pepper
- 2 tablespoons cilantro leaves, finely sliced
- 4 tablespoons sliced chives or scallions

Condiments Optional

- 4 tablespoons diced chili vinegar
- 2 teaspoons dried Kee Noo chili flakes
- 4 tablespoons crushed red chili vinegar
- 2 teaspoons sweet black bean sauce or sweet soy sauce

Place one tablespoon of olive oil and reserved shrimp shells in a small skillet over medium heat and sauté for about 2 to 3 minutes until shrimp shells turn red and set aside.

Place stock ingredients into a large stockpot over high heat and bring to a boil. Add cooked shrimp shells and bring to a boil. Reduce heat to low and simmer until stock reduces by half. Strain stock in a colander and keep warm at low heat.

Place thick lean bacon into a frying pan over low heat and cook until bacon turns crispy, break into small pieces and set aside. Blanch shrimp, crabmeat, fish balls and fish cakes in boiling water for $1^{1}/_{2}$ to 2 minutes, remove and set aside.

Blanch egg noodles and bean sprouts in same boiling water for 1 to $1^{1}/_{2}$ minutes. Remove and place into 4 separate noodle soup bowls. Divide shrimp, crabmeat, fish balls and fish cakes on top of noodles. Add remaining ingredients over the seafood. Sprinkle crispy bacon on top and pour shrimp stock over noodles. ❖

The first time that I arrived in Thailand with my mother and father, Sandi and Tommy Tang, and my older sister Aisha, it was extremely hot and humid — we could hardly take it. The thing that made it even worse was it that it was April, one of the hottest months in Thailand. We went to many places in Thailand, Hong Kong, and then back to Thailand again. Finally, we went to my favorite place in Thailand, Phuket Island. Phuket has a very good environment. The fresh air and the clean waters are amazing. When my sister and I first went on to the beach we thought that we would be tanning on a typical LA beach, but when we first stepped on the sand and took our first look at the ocean we dropped everything in our hands, we were so happy to be there! My family spent 24-7 on the beach. Phuket has the most beautiful surroundings. My family and I stayed at the Club Andaman Beach Resort, a beautiful hotel on the beach. We had the best view. We love staying in Phuket, it's our favorite place to go. There are so many good things to say about it and its sparkling beaches. There is not one piece of trash or any type of pollution on the ground or in the air. It's completely pollutant free and rude people free. We love going to Phuket, and if you want to have fun, go there too.

Chyna Tang

China Town, Bangkok.

ห้างขายทอง
ฮั้วเซ่งเฮง
和
成
興
大
金
行
WHITE ORCHID HOTEL
จอดรถ 24 ชม.
เลี่ยงเซ่งเฮง

NOODLES

*T*he city of Guang-Zhou, better known by most people as Canton, is located in Goung-Dong province, in The People's Republic of China.

I went to China in June 2000 for the first time to scout locations for my TV travels and cooking show. As you know, my show starts out on location exploring the city, culture, history and cuisine. On this scouting trip, I was very interested to find more noodle specialty dishes. One evening, at a banquet hosted by the deputy director of the Guang-Zhou Tourism Bureau, Mr. Ma Xiang Cheng, I asked him, what are the most famous noodles in Guang-Zhou? He told our guide/translator, of course "Boat Noodles". Now you are talking Mr. Ma, I would love to try them. Before I could finish my sentence, he said, would you like to go now? Oh! No, thank you, Mr. Ma, maybe next time when we come back here to tape the show. Would you kindly take me then? We toasted to good health and the banquet started.

I returned to Guang-Zhou, to tape my TV show in January 2001. I phoned Mr. Ma, and asked him about the Boat Noodles that we discussed last time I was here. He didn't remember what I was talking about, "Boat Noodles?" Maybe we had too much to drink that night. With help from my new tour guide, we found out that my last translator had misinformed me. What Mr. Ma really said was "Hor-Fhun", (Hor means river and Fhun means rice). I'm more confused, "River Rice"? Now would someone please explain to me what all this is about? Our new guide put it this way, we call it Hor Fhun and it means noodles made from white rice. Well, that is not all; he also told me, "There is a city near the river and their most famous food is rice noodles and also is the birthplace of rice noodles. Oy-vey! This is unbelievable, I'm looking for some famous noodle dish for my TV show, and how lucky can I get to stumble on the Birthplace of *Rice Noodles*.

My new guide, Thomas, took me to Fha Huer city the next evening for dinner. Fha Huer district is located 30 miles outside of Guang-Zhou city. This district is the Birthplace of Rice Noodles. When we arrived at the Fha Huer Hotel & Restaurant to have dinner, the owner invited me to see how they made rice noodles the old-fashioned way. (I guessed Thomas told them, I work with Public Television.) This restaurant is the only place left in Guang-Zhou that still makes rice noodles the way they did thousands of years ago. I was very fortunate to go down to the basement of the restaurant and see the old equipment that still makes fresh rice noodles. There are many varieties of rice noodles, from the flat style, that looks like ribbons, to fettuccini, linguine size, strings and strands. Noodles may come in triangular or square shapes or large sheets to hold stuffing. Some are very thin and similar to angel hair pasta. There are many ways to cook them and thousands of recipes to duplicate.

For you Rice Noodle fanatics, if you have a chance to go to Guang-Zhou, please be sure to make the pilgrimage yourself. After all, you have been eating them for years...

Tommy

Crispy Noodle Shrimp with Bamboo Shoot Sauce

This is a noodle dish that my father likes to eat when he can't decide whether to order Duck Noodle Soup or Crispy Noodle Shrimp. In the restaurant they make it with chicken but my father likes it with shrimp, so shrimp it is!

❖ *Recipe serves 4*

- 1 lb. crispy egg noodles (see page 193 for instructions)
- 3 tablespoons olive oil
- 1 tablespoon finely chopped garlic
- 2 cups bamboo shoot strips (see glossary page 202)
- $\frac{1}{2}$ cup shredded carrots
- $\frac{1}{2}$ cup fresh or dried soaked shiitake mushrooms, sliced into $\frac{1}{4}$ inch strips
- 4 cups chicken or vegetable stock (see page 195)
- $\frac{1}{2}$ lb. medium shrimp, shelled and deveined
- $2\frac{1}{2}$ tablespoons Thai fish sauce seasoning
- $1\frac{1}{2}$ tablespoons Thai light soy sauce
- 2 tablespoons roasted sesame oil
- 1 tablespoon sugar
- 1 teaspoon ground white pepper
- 2 tablespoons rice vinegar
- 4 tablespoons tapioca flour, corn starch or all purpose flour
- $\frac{1}{2}$ cup cold water
- $\frac{1}{2}$ cup sliced scallions, 1 inch in length
- $\frac{1}{2}$ cup sliced cilantro or Italian parsley leaves
- 1 tablespoon red chili vinegar (see page 190 for instructions) (optional)

Divide crispy egg noodles evenly in four large pasta bowls and set aside.

Place olive oil and garlic into a large deep skillet over high heat and stir until garlic turns light brown. Add bamboo shoots and carrots, stir for 1 minute. Add shiitake mushrooms and chicken stock, stir and bring sauce to a boil. Add shrimp, fish sauce, soy sauce, sesame oil, sugar, white pepper and vinegar and bring sauce to a boil. Mix tapioca flour and water together and stir until thoroughly blended and add into boiling sauce. Stir constantly until sauce becomes thick like gravy. Add scallions and stir for 30 seconds. Remove and pour shrimp with bamboo shoot sauce over crispy egg noodles and sprinkle with cilantro leaves.

Have a puffy noodle day! ❖

Chicken Noodles with Mushroom Sauce

When you prepare this recipe, the crispy Mee-Krob noodles on the plates looks like a lot and you may wonder how you're going to finish it. Well just wait, as soon as you pour the mushroom sauce over the crispy noodles, it shrinks to almost nothing. You should eat it right away before the crispy noodles become too soft. To hear the crunch sound in your mouth is part of the fun. Add diced chili vinegar and chili flakes, if you like it hot.

❖ *Recipe serves 4*

Marinade

- 3 tablespoons tapioca flour
- 3 tablespoons oyster sauce
- 2 tablespoons roasted sesame oil
- 1 tablespoons rice vinegar
- 2 teaspoons sugar
- 1 tablespoon salt-free Thai seasoning
- 12 oz. chicken breast sliced into $1\frac{1}{2}$ inch strips

Sauce

- 3 tablespoons olive oil
- $1\frac{1}{2}$ tablespoons finely chopped garlic
- 3 tablespoons bean condiment (see glossary page 202)
- 16 whole dried shiitake mushrooms
- 5 cups warm water, for soaking mushrooms
- $\frac{3}{4}$ cup thinly julienned carrots
- 2 cups fresh or dried oyster mushrooms cut into small pieces
- 1 cup sliced red bell pepper
- $\frac{1}{2}$ tablespoon sweet black bean sauce
- 3 tablespoon Thai fish sauce seasoning
- 1 tablespoon rice vinegar
- 1 tablespoon sugar
- 1 teaspoon ground white pepper
- 1 tablespoon roasted white sesame seeds
- 5 cups water
- 4 cups Asian broccoli cut into small pieces
- 1 teaspoon sea salt
- 8 oz. Crispy Mee Krob noodles (see glossary page 193)
- $\frac{1}{2}$ cup small sliced chili vinegar (optional)
- 1 tablespoon Kee Noo chili flakes (optional)

Soak shiitake mushrooms in 5 cups of warm water for 30 minutes or until soft, remove stems, put mushrooms back into water and set aside.

Place marinade ingredients into a mixing bowl, mix thoroughly, add chicken and set aside.

Place olive oil into a large deep skillet over medium high heat. Add garlic and bean condiment and stir for a minute. Add mushrooms and their liquid and bring to a boil. Add marinated chicken and stir constantly to allow marinade mixture to dissolve in mushroom liquid and bring to a boil. Add carrots, oyster mushrooms, bell pepper, black bean sauce, fish sauce, vinegar, and sugar. Stir constantly and bring sauce to a boil until it becomes thick like gravy. Mushroom sauce is ready to be used. Remove and transfer to a large soup bowl. Sprinkle white pepper and sesame seeds on top of the sauce. Keep warm.

Place water and sea salt into a stockpot and bring to boil. Add Asian broccoli and blanch for 2 minutes, drain and removed excess water and transfer to 4 large plates. Arrange crispy noodles on top of blanched Asian broccoli. Serve mushroom sauce over crispy Mee Krob noodles on plates. ❖

Pad Thai Noodles

I wasn't going to include this most famous of Thai noodles in this book. But if I leave it out, many people will scream their lungs out at me. You see, I already included it in my last cookbook, Tommy Tang's Modern Thai Cuisine. So I'm giving in to my family and friends including my kitchen staff. Here it is, the Pad Thai noodles that everyone has to order when they visit Tommy Tang's Restaurant. Now you can prepare these noodles for your kid's school lunch. It's very good, even when cold and your children will enjoy it.

❖ *Recipe serves 4*

12 oz. soft Pad Thai noodles (Sen Chen, see page 194 for instruction)	3 tablespoons Thai fish sauce seasoning
4 tablespoons olive or vegetable oil	2 tablespoons honey or sugar
1 tablespoon chopped garlic	1 tablespoon paprika
1 lb. medium shrimp, shelled and deveined	1/2 teaspoon Kee Noo chili (optional)
2 tablespoons dried baby shrimp (optional)	1/2 cup crushed unsalted peanuts
1/2 cup small diced firm white or brown tofu	2 cups fresh bean sprouts
2 eggs beaten	3 tablespoons sliced scallions
1/2 cup tamarind juice (see page 197)	1/4 cup thinly julienned leeks
3 tablespoons rice or white vinegar	4 sprigs cilantro

Place olive oil and garlic in a large skillet over medium heat and sauté until garlic lightly browned. Add shrimp and tofu and turn heat to high and sauté for 1 to 2 minutes. Add beaten eggs and stir gently for 30 seconds. Add tamarind juice, vinegar, fish sauce, honey, paprika, Kee Noo chili and stir for a minute. Add soft Pad Thai noodles and stir constantly for 3 to 4 minutes. Add half of the crushed peanuts, bean sprouts and stir for another 2 minutes. Remove and transfer to a large pasta bowl or platter. Sprinkle with scallions, remaining peanuts, leeks and garnish with cilantro sprigs and serve. ❖

Crab and Shrimp in A Clay Pot

***W**hen I made this dish, instead of using a clay pot I substituted with aluminum foil. All you have to do is create a pocket, large enough to hold the mixture. Make sure that you have at least 3 layers of aluminum foil and it's large enough that you'll be able to fold it closed. After it's done, remove to the plates and with scissors or a sharp knife slit open the top of the aluminum foil. The aroma that gushes out is to die for! Don't stick your nose too close unless you would like to have a red nose like Rudolph the reindeer.*

❖ *Recipe serves 4*

- 3 tablespoons olive oil
- 2 tablespoons garlic finely chopped
- 3 tablespoons crab paste
- 6 pieces sliced ginger $^1/_4$ by 3 inches in length
- 6 roots cilantro
- 8 pieces of crab claws
- 8 large tiger prawns, shells intact (size 11 to 13 per pound)
- 2 cups sliced brown onions
- 2 cups sliced tender celery
- 1 cup shredded carrots
- 12 oz. soft silver noodles (see page 195 for instructions)
- 1$^1/_2$ tablespoons cracked black pepper
- 2 tablespoons Thai fish sauce seasoning
- 3 tablespoons Thai light soy sauce
- 4 cups chicken or vegetable stock
- $^1/_2$ cup thinly sliced red pepper, 3-inch strips
- 2 teaspoons chili oil (see page 190 for instructions)
- 1 cup parsley leaves

Place olive oil and garlic into a large deep skillet over medium heat and stir for a minute. Add crab paste, ginger and cilantro root and stir for a minute. Add crab claws and prawns and stir for 2 minutes. Add brown onions, celery, carrots and silver noodles and stir for 1 minute. Add black pepper, fish sauce, soy sauce, chicken stock and stir for a minute.

Remove and transfer to 2 large clay pots and sprinkle with red bell pepper, chili oil, and parsley and cover.

Place clay pots into a pre-heated oven at 375 degrees and bake for 15 to 17 minutes. Remove and serve as one of multiple courses or on its own with cooked Thai jasmine rice. ❖

Garlic Noodles with Organic Fresh Mint

I would suggest bringing your toothbrush with you after you eat these garlicky noodles. Don't toss the mint sprigs away. You may like to have them for safety in case you have a hot date. For you garlic lovers, this is to die for! Now, let's get the vampire.

❖ *Recipe serves 4*

- 12 oz. dried Asian noodles or angel hair pasta
- 8 cups water
- $^1/_2$ teaspoon sea salt
- 3 tablespoons virgin olive oil
- 4 tablespoons finely chopped garlic
- 1 tablespoons roasted sesame oil
- 1$^1/_2$ tablespoons Thai fish sauce seasoning or $^1/_2$ teaspoon sea salt
- $^1/_4$ teaspoon Kee Noo chili flakes
- 1 teaspoon ground white pepper
- 1 teaspoon sugar
- 2 tablespoons fresh lemon or lime juice
- $^1/_2$ cup thinly sliced fresh organic mint leaves
- $^1/_2$ cup finely diced red bell pepper
- $^1/_2$ cup thinly sliced chives or scallions
- 1 cup crispy shallots (see page 192 for instructions)
- 12 chives or young scallions for garnish
- 4 sprigs fresh organic mint leaves for garnish

Soak Asian noodles in cold water for 10 minutes, drain and set aside. Place water and salt into a stockpot over high heat and bring to a boil. Add noodles and cook for 2-3 minutes, drain and rinse with cold water and set aside. (If you use angel hair pasta, cook pasta for 3-4 minutes)

Place olive oil and garlic into a sauce pan over medium heat and sauté garlic for 2 to 3 minutes or until garlic turns light golden brown. Remove and transfer garlic olive oil to a large mixing bowl. Add roasted sesame oil and set aside. Allow infused garlic olive oil to completely cool before using. Add fish sauce, chili flakes, white pepper, sugar and lemon juice. Whisk the mixture until thoroughly blended.

Place cold noodles and sliced mint leaves into a mixing bowl and toss noodles until thoroughly coated with sauce. Transfer noodles to a large serving plate and sprinkle with red bell pepper, crispy shallots, diced chives and garnish with long chives and mint leaves sticking up in the center mound of garlic noodles. ❖

Guang-Zhou Noodles

Guang-Zhou City is the birthplace of rice noodles. There are thousands of ways to cook these noodles. Each city around the globe has its own version and recipes. This recipe is easy and simple to do. I splash on chili oil to spice it up a notch and that is the Thai way.

❖ *Recipe serves 4*

- 4 tablespoons olive oil
- 1 tablespoon chopped garlic
- $^1/_2$ cup sliced onions
- $^1/_2$ cup sliced red bell pepper
- $^1/_2$ cup thinly sliced tender celery
- 1 lb. fresh flat rice noodles or dried Rad-Na noodles (see page 195 for instructions)
- $^1/_4$ cup light soy sauce
- 1 tablespoon roasted sesame oil
- 3 tablespoons rice vinegar
- 2 teaspoons sugar
- $^1/_2$ cup Chinese chive flowers
- 2 cups fresh bean sprouts
- 4 tablespoons sliced scallions
- 4 tablespoons ground unsalted peanuts
- 1 teaspoon ground white pepper
- 1 tablespoon chili oil

Place olive oil and garlic into a large frying pan or wok, over high heat. Add onions, red bell pepper and celery and stir for a minute. Add flat noodles and stir for 2 to 3 minutes. Add soy sauce, sesame oil, vinegar, sugar and stir for 2 minutes. Add chive flowers, bean sprouts, scallions, ground peanuts and white pepper, stirring constantly for a minute. Remove and transfer to a large platter and splash with chili oil. ❖

● **Chestnut vendors in Bangkok.**

Polish Sausage with Santa Fe Chili Noodles

In the early days, many immigrants from Italy, Germany and Poland migrated to Buffalo, NY to work in the steel industry, which is no longer there. With them, they brought their ethnic cuisine, and sausage is part of their pride. When I was experimenting with different kind of sausages in Angola, near Buffalo, my buddy, Al Jr, son of Al Sr., walked in the kitchen, and said "Try this Kiel-ba-sa sausage." I said "What kind of sausage?" "Kiel-ba-sa," he said, "you can call it Polish sausage." Polish sausage, um, sounds good. Thanks dad, for your kind assistance.

❖ *Recipe serves 4*

- 4 links fresh Polish sausage, 7 inches in length
- 6 tablespoons virgin olive oil
- 2 tablespoons chopped garlic
- 1 cup sliced red bell pepper
- 1 cup sliced yellow bell pepper
- 1 cup sliced Anaheim chili pepper
- 1/2 cup shredded carrots
- 1 1/2 cups sliced brown onions
- 2 teaspoons Santa Fe chili powder
- 3 tablespoons Thai fish sauce seasoning
- 3 tablespoons rice vinegar
- 1 teaspoon roasted cracked black pepper
- 1 teaspoon Kee Noo chili flakes
- 1/2 cup vegetable, chicken stock or water
- 12 oz. soft Mee Krob noodles (see page 194 for instructions)
- 1/4 cup thinly sliced leeks
- 1/2 cup fresh oregano leaves
- 1 cup crispy leeks (see page 193 for instructions)
- 4 pieces lime or lemon wedges
- 1/2 cup crispy shallots (see page 192 for instructions)

Place 4 Polish sausage links into a skillet over medium heat and sear for 20 to 25 minutes. Turn occasionally to brown all sides, remove and slice at a 45 degree angle, half an inch thick and two inches in length and set aside.

Place olive oil and garlic into a large deep skillet over high heat and stir for a minute. Add red and yellow bell peppers, Anaheim chili, carrots and onions and stir for 2 to 3 minutes. Add Santa Fe chili powder, fish sauce, vinegar, black pepper, Kee Noo chili and vegetable stock, stir for a minute and add soft Mee Krob noodles. Stir constantly for 3 to 4 minutes and remove to a large platter, sprinkle with leeks and oregano. Place crispy shallots and leeks on top and arrange seared Polish sausage around the plate. Squeeze juice from lime wedges, if desired. ❖

Roasted Chili Noodles with Sage

When I don't know what to cook, I can always start with a jar of Thai roasted chili paste and go from there. You can use any type of noodle but I prefer to use Rad-Na noodles for this recipe. Adding fresh sage gives it another dimension. If you can't find sage, by all means switch to basil or mint. But whatever the herb, it should be fresh.

❖ *Recipe serves 4*

- 1/4 cup olive oil
- 1 tablespoon finely chopped fresh garlic
- 2 tablespoons Thai roasted chili paste
- 1/2 cup sliced brown onions
- 3/4 cup julienned carrots
- 1 cup sliced red bell pepper
- 3/4 cup thinly sliced celery
- 1 cup diced tomatoes
- 1 1/2 tablespoons Thai fish sauce seasoning
- 8 oz. soft Rad-Na noodles (see glossary page 195)
- 8 oz. Canadian bacon cut in strips
- 1/2 cup vegetable or chicken stock
- 1 cup sliced scallions, 1 inch long
- 4 cups bean sprouts
- 1 teaspoon ground white pepper
- 2 tablespoons sliced fresh sage
- 1 teaspoon Kee Noo chili flakes (optional)

Place olive oil and garlic into a large skillet over high heat and stir for a minute. Add roasted chili paste and sauté for a minute. Add brown onions, carrots, red bell pepper, celery, tomatoes and Thai fish sauce and stir for a minute. Add Rad-Na noodles, Canadian bacon strips and vegetable stock. Stir constantly for 3 to 4 minutes to make sure noodles do not stick to the skillet. Add bean sprouts, scallions, white pepper and fresh sage (or basil or mint) and stir for 2 minutes. Remove roasted chili noodles to a serving platter, sprinkle with Thai chili flakes. ❖

● Chinese New Year Celebration.

Pho Tree Noodles

May is an important month for Thais and Vesakha Day is the most important day for Buddhists. All over the world Buddhists celebrate the three events in Buddha's life that happened in May. Vesakha Day is when Buddha was born, reached supreme enlightenment and passed away. One of his teachings is to have Character, Charity and Compassion for humans and other living beings. That includes trees, I suppose. We should eat to survive, not survive just to eat. He never taught people to be vegetarians, but rather let us choose to walk the middle path and be compassionate to others.

So, Vesakha Day is my Veggie Day.

❖ *Recipe serves 4*

- 4 tablespoons olive or vegetable oil
- 1 cup diced white or yellow tofu (see glossary page 203)
- 1 tablespoon finely chopped garlic
- 1/2 cup sliced shiitake mushrooms
- 12 oz. soft Mee Krob noodles (see page 194 for instructions)
- 1/2 cup carrots thinly julienned
- 1 cup vegetable stock (see page 195 for instructions)
- 1/4 cup Thai light soy sauce
- 1/4 cup rice vinegar
- 1 teaspoon ground white pepper
- 1 cup thinly sliced red bell pepper
- 4 whole thinly sliced Serrano chili
- 2/3 cup crispy shallots (see page 192 for instructions)
- 1/2 cup crispy ginger (see page 193 for instructions)
- 4 oz. crispy silver noodles (see page 194 for instructions)
- 4 tablespoons roasted sesame seeds
- 1/2 cup small sliced scallions
- 3/4 cup parsley leaves
- 2 teaspoons dried Kee Noo chili flakes (optional)
- 1 tablespoon crushed red chili vinegar

Place 2 tablespoons of olive oil into a large skillet over medium high heat. Add tofu and cook until it turns crispy and golden brown, then remove and set aside. Add remaining oil to skillet. Add garlic and mushrooms and stir for a minute. Add noodles and carrots and stir constantly for 2-3 minutes. Add half a cup of stock, soy sauce and vinegar. Stir for 2 to 3 minutes. Add white pepper, red bell pepper, Serrano chili and (if noodles are too dry) remaining vegetable stock, stirring constantly for 3 minutes. Remove to 4 serving plates. Sprinkle shallots, and ginger over cooked noodles. Arrange crispy silver noodles in the shape of a tree on the top.

Toss sesame seeds and scallions around the noodle tree and arrange some parsley leaves around crispy noodle tree and around the entire plate.

Have a peaceful Veggie Day! ❖

Scott Chow Fun

Whenever I visit New York City, I always have dinner with my dear friend, Scott, in his apartment. It is our ritual that we do on the day I arrive in town. We always order take out from the local restaurants. No matter how many take-out menus we look at, you can bet that we will end up with Chinese food and Chow Fun as part of our meal. It is our tradition that we have to have it!

Scott, this is for you.

❖ *Recipe Serves 4*

Marinade

- 8 oz. thin sliced fillet of beef 1 by 2 inch strips
- 1 tablespoon roasted sesame oil
- 1 tablespoon oyster sauce
- $\frac{1}{2}$ teaspoon ground white pepper
- $\frac{1}{2}$ teaspoon sugar

Noodles

- 3 tablespoons olive or vegetable oil
- 1 tablespoon chopped garlic
- 2 tablespoons bean condiment (see glossary page 202)
- 12 oz. fresh rice noodles (see glossary page 204)
- 4 cups *Asian broccoli
- 1 cup sliced brown onions
- 3 tablespoons sliced, peeled fresh ginger cut into thin $1\frac{1}{4}$ inch strips
- $\frac{1}{2}$ cup sliced bamboo shoots
- 2 tablespoons Thai fish sauce seasoning
- 2 tablespoons Thai sweet black bean sauce (sweet soy sauce)
- 2 tablespoons Thai light soy sauce
- 2 tablespoons rice or vegetable vinegar
- 2 teaspoons sugar
- $\frac{1}{2}$ teaspoon ground white pepper
- $\frac{1}{2}$ cup sliced scallions $1\frac{1}{2}$ inches in length
- 2 cups fresh bean sprouts
- 2 tablespoons diced chili vinegar (optional) (see page 190 for instructions)
- 1 teaspoon dried Kee Noo chili flakes (optional)

Place beef and marinade ingredients together in a bowl, mix thoroughly and set aside. Heat 1 tablespoon of oil in a large skillet over high heat. Add marinated beef and leave undisturbed in the skillet for a minute, stir beef for another 1-2 minutes or until it's semi-cooked. Transfer beef to the same mixing bowl and set aside.

Place remaining oil into the same large skillet over high heat, add garlic and bean condiment and stir for a minute. Add rice noodles and stir for 2 minutes. Add semi-cooked beef, broccoli, ginger, bamboo shoots and stir for 2 to 3 minutes. Add remaining ingredients except the scallions and the bean sprouts, stirring gently and constantly for 3 minutes. Add scallions and bean sprouts and stir until ingredients are thoroughly mixed. Transfer to a large serving plate and sprinkle with ground white pepper. Add diced chili vinegar and chili flakes as desired.

*Asian broccoli : cut leaves into small pieces and peel hard fiber parts off broccoli stem and cut lengthwise. ❖

Singapore Noodles

This is probably the noodle dish that everybody has to order when they go to a Singapore-style Chinese restaurant, You order Singapore noodles just like you would order Pad Thai noodles when you go to a Thai restaurant. This is a very simple recipe and you can make it vegetarian by omitting meats and seafood. You also can add or substitute anything you like to it, but you can't omit noodles and curry powder.

❖ *Recipe serves 4*

- 1/3 cup olive or vegetable oil
- 1 1/2 tablespoons finely chopped garlic
- 1 1/2 cups sliced smoked ham or Canadian, bacon 1/4 by 1 1/2 inch strips
- 3/4 lb. shrimp size 26-30 lb., shelled and deveined
- 1/2 cup shredded carrots
- 1 cup thinly sliced celery
- 1 cup sliced brown onions
- 1/2 cup thinly sliced red bell pepper
- 1 1/4 tablespoons curry powder
- 3 tablespoons Thai fish sauce seasoning
- 1/4 cup rice vinegar
- 10 oz. soft Mee Krob noodles (see page 194)
- 1/2 cup vegetarian stock or fresh water
- 1/4 cup sliced cilantro leaves
- 1 cup shredded scallion strips 2-2 1/2 inches in length
- 1 1/2 teaspoons ground white pepper
- 1 tablespoon chili oil

Place olive oil and garlic into a large skillet over high heat and stir for a minute. Add ham and shrimp and stir for 1 minute. Add carrots, celery, onion, bell pepper and curry powder and stir for a minute. Add fish sauce, vinegar and noodles and stir for 2 minutes. Add stock or water and stir constantly for 3 to 4 minutes. Remove to a large platter, garnish with cilantro and scallions. Sprinkle with white pepper and chili oil. ❖

• China Town @ night.

Peking Noodles

I should call this dish Beijing Noodles to be politically correct but I'm an old fashioned guy and I like the old name Peking. It sounds better. If you live far away from an Asian market, you may substitute spaghetti for Lo Mein noodles.

❖ *Recipe serves 4*

Marinade

- 1 whole skinless duck breast sliced into small strips
- 2 tablespoons Hoisin sauce
- 2 tablespoons finely chopped garlic
- 3 tablespoons roasted sesame oil
- 1 tablespoon ground black pepper

Noodles

- 8 cups water
- 1 teaspoon sea salt
- 10 oz. *Fresh Chinese Lo Mein egg noodles
- 4 tablespoons olive or vegetable oil
- 3 tablespoons thinly julienned, peeled fresh ginger 1$^{1}/_{4}$ inches in length
- 1 cup sliced brown onions
- $^{1}/_{4}$ cup white wine
- 3 tablespoons Thai light soy sauce
- 3 tablespoons rice vinegar
- 1$^{1}/_{2}$ tablespoons Thai fish sauce seasoning
- $^{1}/_{2}$ cup thinly sliced red bell pepper
- $^{1}/_{3}$ cup julienned carrots
- $^{1}/_{2}$ cup vegetable stock or fresh water
- $^{3}/_{4}$ cup sliced scallions cut 1 inch in length
- $^{1}/_{4}$ cup Italian parsley leaves (flat leaf parsley)
- 1 teaspoon ground white pepper
- 1 teaspoon Kee Noo chili flakes (optional)

Place duck and marinade ingredients into a bowl, mix thoroughly and set aside. Place water and salt into a large stockpot over high heat and bring to a boil. Add egg noodles and blanch for 1 minute. Drain and rinse in cold water and set aside.

Place oil into a large skillet over high heat, add marinated duck and stir for 3 minutes. Add noodles, ginger, brown onions and stir for 1 to 2 minutes. Add white wine, soy sauce, fish sauce and vinegar and stir for a minute. Add bell pepper, carrots and vegetable stock, stirring constantly for 3 to 4 minutes. Add scallions and keep stirring for another minute. Remove and transfer to a large serving platter. Sprinkle with parsley and white pepper and chili flakes if you like.

* To cook spaghetti bring 8 cups of water to a boil in a medium stockpot. Add 8 oz. spaghetti and $^{1}/_{2}$ teaspoon sea salt and cook for 12 to 14 minutes, (noodles have to be soft to use in this recipe) remove, let it cool and set aside. ❖

Vegetarian Lo-Mein

I believe that all Cantonese Chinese restaurants serve these noodles. There are so simple to prepare and they are a safe dish if you are not sure what to order. You can buy Lo-Mein already steamed and you can also add shrimp, chicken, pork or beef to it. Or better yet, you can add them all and name this dish after yourself.

❖ *Recipe serves 4*

- 10 oz. *Fresh Chinese Lo-Mein noodles (it's a long round noodle $^{1}/_{8}$ inch thick)
- 8 cups water
- 1 teaspoon sea salt
- 2 tablespoons roasted sesame oil
- 4 tablespoons olive or vegetable oil
- 1 tablespoon finely chopped garlic
- 3 tablespoons thinly julienned, peeled fresh ginger $1^{1}/_{4}$ inches in length
- 1 cup sliced brown onions
- $^{3}/_{4}$ cup sliced bamboo shoots
- 3 tablespoons Thai light soy sauce
- $1^{1}/_{2}$ tablespoons Thai fish sauce seasoning
- 3 tablespoons rice vinegar
- $^{1}/_{2}$ cup thinly sliced red bell pepper
- $1^{1}/_{2}$ cups thinly shredded green cabbage
- $^{1}/_{2}$ cup vegetable stock or fresh water
- $^{3}/_{4}$ cup sliced scallions cut 1 inch in length
- $1^{1}/_{2}$ teaspoons ground white pepper

Place water and salt into a large stockpot over high heat and bring to a boil. Add Lo-Mein noodles and blanch for 2 to 3 minutes. Drain and rinse in cold water. After noodles dry, add sesame oil and toss until noodles are thoroughly coated and set aside.

Place oil and garlic into a large skillet over high heat and stir for a minute. Add ginger, brown onion and bamboo shoots and stir for 1 to 2 minutes. Add soy sauce, fish sauce and vinegar and stir for a minute. Add cooked noodles, bell pepper and cabbage, stirring constantly for 4 minutes. Add stock and scallions and keep stirring for 2-3 minutes. Transfer to a serving platter and sprinkle with white pepper.

*If you are using steamed Lo-Mein, it's not necessary to blanch the noodles. ❖

Thai Angel Hair Pasta with Pineapple Shrimp Sauce

This style of noodles is a snack to hold you over between meals. I prefer to have it on a hot summer day. The sweetness of the pineapple and acidity from the tomatoes gives a cooling sensation ... until you bite on the crispy Kee Noo chilis. Your mouth becomes warm from the chili heat. The heat gets intensifies until the next scoop of Pineapple Shrimp Sauce. The commotion goes on and on until you finish the plate and the heat remains, because there is no more sauce left. Help! The street pineapple vendor is on the way, you buy a slice of cold pineapple that's been sitting on a bed of ice. Ah! What a pineapple day....

❖ *Recipe serves 4*

- 4 dried Kee Noo or Serrano chilies, seeded and soaked in 1/4 cup warm water for 1/2 hour or until soft
- 1/4 cup chopped red bell pepper
- 2 cups coarsely chopped fresh pineapple (substitute with canned pineapple with no sugar or syrup added)
- 1/2 cup sliced shallots
- 1/2 teaspoon sea salt
- 1 teaspoon palm sugar
- 1 cup cherry tomatoes cut in half
- 2 teaspoons Thai fish sauce seasoning
- 1 cup water
- 1 cup minced raw shrimp (about 1/2 lb.)
- 2 tablespoons chopped Italian parsley
- 8 oz. Kha Nom Jeen noodles (same as somen noodles) "angel hair pasta size"
- 1/2 teaspoon sea salt
- 5 cups ice-cold water
- 2 tablespoons sliced chives
- 2 cups fresh bean sprouts
- 1/2 cup crispy shallots (see page 192 for instructions)
- 12 crispy Kee Noo chilies

Combine soft Kee Noo chilies and red bell pepper in a blender and blend until smooth. Transfer the mixture to a deep skillet over high heat and bring to a boil. Add pineapple, shallots, sea salt, and palm sugar, stir and bring to a boil. Add cherry tomatoes, fish sauce, and water and bring sauce to a boil. Reduce heat to low and simmer for 3 to 4 minutes. Add minced shrimp and bring sauce to a boil. Reduce heat to low and simmer for another 4 to 5 minutes or until sauce become semi-thick. Remove, stir in chopped parsley and let it cool.

Place water and salt into a medium stockpot over high heat and bring to a boil. Add Kha Nom Jeen noodles and cook for 3 minutes. Remove from heat, drain and transfer to ice-cold water. Remove noodles by hand from water, drain and form a baseball-size ball of noodles and put on a plate lined with paper towels. If you are using capellini pasta, cook only 2 minutes. Place cold noodle balls on 4 serving plates and pour pineapple shrimp sauce over noodles. Sprinkle with sliced chives and serve with crispy Kee Noo chilies and crispy shallots as a condiment. ❖

Stir Fried Soba Noodles

My old friend, Henry, introduced me to Soba noodles. He had been living in Tokyo, Japan for three years. When he came to the U.S., he took me to lunch at a Japanese noodle shop. He ordered cold noodles that came on a bamboo mat tray. He told me, you should try these cold noodles, they're called Soba, they're made from buckwheat, and it is healthy for you. Well, all I have to hear is healthy and I can't wait for my first taste of cold Soba. You can also stir-fry these noodles.

❖ *Recipe serves 4*

- 10 oz. soba noodles
- 8 cups water
- 1/2 teaspoon sea salt
- 12 whole dried shiitake mushrooms
- 3 tablespoons virgin olive oil
- 1 tablespoon finely chopped garlic
- 1 cup sliced brown onions
- 1/2 cup sliced red bell pepper
- 1/3 cup shredded carrots
- 1/4 cup thinly julienned, peeled fresh ginger
- 2 tablespoons sesame oil
- 1 tablespoon Thai fish sauce seasoning
- 2 tablespoons Thai light soy sauce
- 1 1/2 teaspoons black pepper
- 1/2 teaspoon Kee Noo chili flakes
- 2 cups crispy wonton skin strips or crispy Mee Krob noodles (see page 194)
- 2 tablespoons toasted sesame seeds
- 4 tablespoons finely sliced scallions

Place shiitake mushrooms in lukewarm water for a half-hour or until tender and slice into 1/4 inch strips, discard stem and set aside.

Place water and salt into a stockpot over high heat and bring to a boil. Add soba noodles and cook for 5 minutes or until tender. Drain and rinse with ice-cold water and set aside.

Place olive oil and garlic into a large skillet over high heat and stir for 1 minute. Add Shiitake mushrooms, onions, bell pepper, carrots and ginger and stir constantly for 2 minutes. Add soba noodles, sesame oil and stir constantly for 2 minutes. Add fish sauce, soy sauce black pepper and chili flakes and keep stirring for 2 to 3 minutes. Remove cooked soba to a large platter and sprinkle with crispy won ton strips, sesame seeds and scallions.

Kum-Pai! ❖

Rice paddy around Ayutthaya.

RICE

My dearest Mom once told me, **"A grain of rice can save your life"** and then she went on and told me a story.

Once upon a time there was a filthy rich boy. He was so rich that he thought he was god and nothing could ever to happen to him. He was born to a kind, rich, business mogul. The boy had no respect for anyone or anything including the food he ate. He would order their cook to make many dishes for him. He just picked at the food and told the maid to throw the rest away. He didn't even have the heart to give leftovers to the poor. No matter how many times his father and mother told him not to waste the food, he didn't listen. They told him, if you keep throwing the rice away, one day you may have nothing to eat. He just ignored them. They loved him so much, and because he was their only child they didn't want to upset him.

As time went on, his parents passed away and left him the fortune and their business to run. Because he was so spoiled and hated school, he never learned anything from class and especially nothing about his father's business. Since he didn't know anything about the business, when the loyal employees that worked with his father tried to guide him, instead he listened to some others who only talked nice to him but didn't care about the business. Eventually, they cheated him out of everything and ran his business into the ground.

He lost the business that his father built, all the money and his beautiful home. He had no place to live and became homeless. Every day he had to search the trash bin for some leftover food. One day a famine hit his hometown, many people had no food to eat and there was no leftover food in the trash. He walked from city to city to find food. Some days he found some and some days he went hungry with nothing in his stomach. One day after walking many miles, he was completely exhausted. Suddenly he spotted a grain of rice on the street in a mud puddle. Somehow this single grain of rice magically managed to float on top of the puddle. He looked at it with wide eyes and walked closer to it. He kneeled down to pick up the rice. Before his hand reached the rice, his eyes connected with another pair of eyes that belonged to a skinny dog. But the dog had no energy left to get the rice. The dog looked at him with very sad eyes. He looked at the dog again and tears were running down his cheeks. He picked up the rice and walked to where the dog sat. He said, "this is yours, you were here before me and you need it more than I." The dog slowly picked up the single grain of rice with his tongue. He turned, and just before he walked away, he fell and passed out from hunger.

He woke up the next day to find himself in a comfortable bed. He smelled a wonderful scent and he thought he was dead! A voice came from the same direction as the fragrant smell. "Oh! You're awake, you must be hungry, come and have a bowl of rice." He sat there with tear-filled eyes. By giving a single grain of rice to the dying dog, he realized that someone just granted him a second chance at life. Where he passed out was next to a rice paddy and the farmers took him to their house and gave him shelter....

So my Mom always said, "Now! Eat every single rice grain from your plate, don't waste it, there are many hungry children."

The flight attendant suddenly awakens me on my trip to Bangkok; it's now time for dinner to be served. I just had a dream, but this dream was so real. Maybe because I'm on the way home. Yes, I think so. Mom, thank you for the life lesson you taught me when I was young and I miss you too....

Tommy

Chicken Garlic Ginger Rice

People in Thailand would always tell me where the newest and best Garlic Chicken Ginger Rice shops were. They knew that I would travel any place just to try them. After many years of searching, I've found the best is across the street from the wholesale seafood market in Bangkok, on New Road. Their secret is in the sauce. They marinate the sauce overnight before they blend it with the other ingredients. I had a chance to get to know the owner and he gave me his secret, but he definitely left out some key ingredients. After I played with it for a while, this sauce is as good at it gets. You may substitute chicken breast with turkey breast. In Thailand they steam the whole bird. So! Try it.

❖ *Recipe serves 4*

- 4 large chicken breasts, skin intact (2-2 1/2 lbs.)
- 4 cups chicken or vegetable stock (see page 195 for instructions)
- 1/3 cup virgin olive oil
- 12 large cloves garlic, gently smashed with skin intact
- 4 pieces sliced ginger 1/4 inch thick with skin on
- 2 cups Thai Jasmine rice (Thai Hom Mali Rice)
- 1 teaspoon sea salt
- 1/2 teaspoon ground white pepper
- 32 pieces thinly sliced cucumber (hot house or small pickle cuke)

Condiment sauce

- 1/3 cup chopped, peeled fresh ginger
- 2 1/2 tablespoons chopped garlic
- 1 1/2 tablespoons crushed red fresh chili paste (Sambal Oelec)
- 2 1/2 tablespoons chopped cilantro roots, stems or leaves
- 1/3 cup Thai bean condiment
- 1/4 cup vegetable or rice vinegar
- 1/4 cup sweet black bean sauce or soy sauce
- 1 tablespoon Thai light soy sauce
- 8 sprigs cilantro (for garnish)

Preheat oven to 425°F.

Place chicken into a deep baking dish skin side up and set aside. Place olive oil and smashed garlic into a deep skillet over medium high heat. Sauté garlic for 1 1/2 to 2 minutes or until it turns light brown. Add ginger and rice and sauté for 2 minutes. Add stock, salt and ground white pepper and stir until rice is mixed thoroughly. Pour rice mixture over chicken breasts and cover with a lid or aluminum foil. Transfer to a preheated oven at 425°F and bake for 30 minutes. Stir rice loose while in oven every 10 minutes.

At the same time place sauce ingredients into a blender and blend until smooth. Remove to a sauce bowl and set aside. After rice has baked for 30 minutes, turn off the oven and keep chicken garlic rice in the oven for 10 minutes.

Remove rice from oven and transfer to a large platter. Slice chicken breasts into bite-size pieces and arrange over cooked rice. Arrange cucumber around rice and garnish with cilantro sprigs. Have a nice garlicky day... ❖

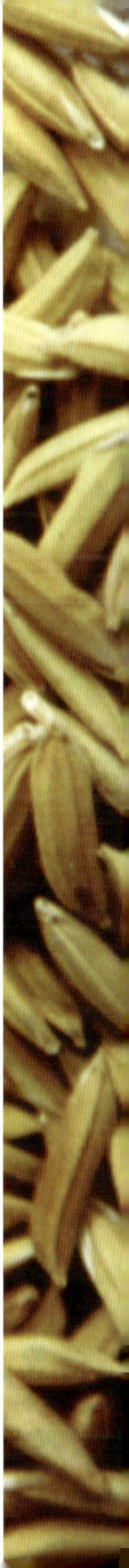

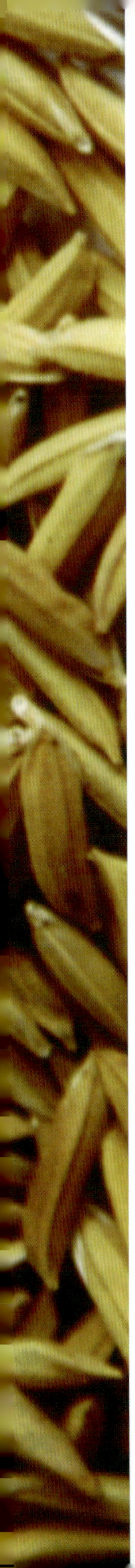

Arabian Nights Chicken & Rice

I went to Palo Verde College in Blythe, California. If you don't know where Blythe is, it is one of the hottest places in summer time. Can you imagine! I had to go to school there. But the people are the nicest people I've ever met. Now, back to why I told you about this city. I met a friend in college and his name is Adul Aziz, who came from Saudi Arabia to study. He and I must have done some-thing wrong in a past life to be punished there. One day Aziz took me to a dinner party at his family home and they served this dish for dinner and I loved it. I loved it so much that I still remembered it as I started to write this book. You see, life is funny sometimes, you think you've been punished, but the reality is that you have a lifetime of a great memories of friends and great food. Here's to you, my lost friend Aziz.

❖ *Recipe serves 4 to 6*

- 6 tablespoons olive oil
- 6 pieces chicken leg quarters (about 3 to 3 1/2 lbs)
- 4 tablespoons curry powder mixture
- 1 1/2 cups coconut milk
- 2 tablespoons chopped garlic
- 2 cups Thai Jasmine rice
- 1 cup finely diced small carrots
- 1 cup diced red bell pepper
- 1 cup sliced brown onions
- 1 cup corn kernels
- 2 tablespoons Thai fish sauce seasoning
- 2 teaspoons sugar
- 4 cups chicken or vegetable stock
- 1/2 cup crispy shallots (see page 192 for instructions)
- 1/4 cup diced Serrano chilies (optional)
- 1/4 cup cilantro leaves (garnish)

Dipping sauce

- 1/2 cup water
- 1/3 cup rice or vegetable vinegar
- 2 tablespoons sugar
- 1/4 teaspoon sea salt
- 1/4 teaspoon fresh red chili paste (see glossary page 202)
- 1 cup diced cucumber (hot house or small pickle cuke)
- 2 tablespoons thinly sliced shallots
- 2 tablespoons sliced cilantro leaves
- 2 tablespoons thinly sliced scallions

Preheat oven to 425°F.

Place one tablespoon of olive oil into a large deep skillet with ovenproof handle over medium high heat. Add chicken and cook for 2-3 minutes. Add 2 tablespoons of curry powder and coconut milk and cook for another 3-4 minutes. Rotate chicken every minute. Remove and set aside.

Place remaining olive oil and garlic into a skillet over high heat, stir for a minute. Add Jasmine rice and stir for 1-2 minutes. Add remaining curry powder, carrots, bell pepper, onions, corn, fish sauce and sugar stirring constantly for 1 minute. Add chicken stock and mix thoroughly. Pour rice mixture over chicken in the large deep skillet and cover with a lid or aluminum foil. Place chicken and rice mixture into the pre-heated oven for 30 minutes. Turn off oven and keep cooked chicken rice warm until ready to serve.

Meanwhile: prepare cucumber-dipping sauce. Place water, vinegar, sugar, sea salt and red chili paste into a saucepan and bring sauce to a boil. Reduce heat to low and simmer for 2 to 3 minutes. Remove and set aside and let it cool. Place cucumber, shallots, cilantro and scallions into a small sauce bowl and pour the cooled sauce over. (Use this sauce as a condiment.)

Remove baked chicken and rice from the oven and place on a serving platter, sprinkle with crispy shallots, diced chili and cilantro. Have a fun Arabian night. ❖

Let me tell you a story about this basil. As you may know, this basil is called Kra-Prao in Thai. Years ago, most Thais knew America as the land of cowboys, hot dogs and apple pie. Rich families who wanted their children to have a Western education would send them to England instead of the U.S. This now has changed, England is too far, too rainy and too cold for most Thais. The option is to send them to India. (India was colonized by Britain and some school educational systems are similar to Britain's, especially in English courses.) Thais love to eat and cook. We like our food tasty and a dish that we can't live without is Kai Kra-Prao.

Once upon a time, there was a group of Thai students who went to study in India. As I mentioned before, Thais love to cook. Therefore, they went to the market in search of the basil they loved most "Kra-Prao", but they couldn't find it. On the way back from the market, they walked by a temple and there was a religious celebration. They all went into the temple to join in the event with the local people to pay their respects to the goddess. They smelled something that was very familiar to them. When they found the source of the scent, Holy behold, they saw many bouquets of Kra-Prao basil in the vase as an offering to the goddess. There was nobody around, so they borrowed some Kra-Prao from the temple, said thanks and asked for forgiveness.

That evening, they cooked dinner and they invited all their Thai and non-Thai friends to join them. A friend asked, "what kind of herb is in this chicken?" It has such a great flavor and aroma! The Thai students looked at each other and before they replied, one of them looked up to the sky and said "Holy Basil". Ah! Holy Basil is a great name for this herb. They all smiled guiltily...

Kai Kra-Prao

Kai Kra-Prao can probably be called one of Thailand's national dishes. I haven't heard anybody ever say they didn't like it. I always introduce this dish to my friends that I take on my Culinary and Cultural tour, and also my TV crew that tapes my PBS Cooking Series for me. They all love it. I prefer to combine minced chicken and minced shrimp in the dish. It gives an extra texture you can't get from chicken alone. Most Thai people like to have it with fried egg; I like my egg extra crispy and the egg yolk turned hard. I then scoop out the egg yolk and give it to whomever I'm eating with. The word Kai means chicken and the word Kra-Prao means holy basil.

❖ *Recipe serves 4*

8 tablespoons olive oil	3 tablespoons Thai fish sauce seasoning
4 whole eggs	2 tablespoons sweet black-bean sauce
4 tablespoons chopped garlic	1 tablespoon rice vinegar
8 whole smashed fresh Kee Noo chilies	2 teaspoons sugar
12 oz. minced chicken breast	$1^1/_4$ cups lemongrass stock (see page 196)
12 oz. finely minced shrimp	1 cup holy basil leaves
2 cups thinly sliced brown onions	6 cups cooked Thai Jasmine rice
1 cup small sliced red bell peppers	(see page 191)

Place oil in a skillet over medium low heat. Crack 1 egg into hot oil and fry until egg turns crispy and egg yolk turns solid. Repeat with remaining eggs. Remove cooked eggs to a plate lined with paper towels to remove excess grease and set aside.

With the same skillet, turn heat to high and add garlic and chili and stir for 1 minute. Add chicken and shrimp and stir for 2 to 3 minutes. Add onions, bell peppers, fish sauce, sweet black bean sauce, vinegar, sugar, and cook for 3-4 minutes. Add lemongrass stock and holy basil and mix thoroughly. Remove and pour over steamy Jasmine rice and place fried eggs on top. ❖

Earth Ocean Wind & Fire

Earth, we don't really know when it will move.
Ocean, we don't know when there will be a flood.
Wind, we don't know when and where it will hit.
Fire, it can happen anywhere.
Earth gives us vegetation and meats.
Ocean gives us water and sealife.
Wind allows us to breathe and to live.
Fire allows us to cook.
They are good and they are bad.
They can give and they can take away.
Either way we cannot live without them.
Don't take things for granted, be gracious and be respectful.

Earth Rice

- 2 cups cooked Thai wild rice (see page 192 for instructions)
- 1/2 cup coconut milk
- 2 tablespoons palm sugar
- 1/2 teaspoon sea salt

Ocean Rice

- 2 cups cooked Jasmine rice (see page 191 for instructions)
- 1/2 cup finely chopped cilantro
- 1/2 teaspoon sea salt
- 1/2 teaspoon granulated garlic
- 1/2 teaspoon ground white pepper

Wind Rice

- 2 cups cooked sticky rice (see page 191 for instructions)
- 1/2 cup coconut milk
- 4 tablespoons sugar
- 1/2 teaspoon sea salt

Fire Rice

- 1 cup cooked Jasmine brown rice (see page 191 for instructions)
- 1 tablespoon Santa Fe chili powder
- 1/2 teaspoon granulated garlic
- 1/2 teaspoon sea salt

Combine ingredients in 4 separate bowls and mix each bowl thoroughly. Transfer each bowl to a serving platter and arrange in a circle. Rice is ready to eat as part of a feast. ❖

Ginger Fried Rice with Shrimp

Ginger is one of the main staples in Thai cuisine. There are many varieties of ginger; white, red, purple to name just a few. But the white ginger is the most commonly used in cooking. The pungent warm soothing flavor gives the dish an exotic taste. When I had a bad cold and stomachache, my Mom used to brew fresh ginger tea for me to drink. She added a little brown sugar to it. When I duplicate this drink for my two girls, I add honey instead of sugar and a few drops of freshly squeezed lemon juice.

❖ *Recipe serves 4*

- 1/3 cup virgin olive oil
- 1/4 cup thinly julienned, peeled fresh ginger 1 1/2 inches in length
- 20 large shrimp shelled and deveined
- 2 tablespoons finely chopped garlic
- 1/4 cup peeled finely chopped, fresh ginger
- 6 cups cooked Jasmine rice (see page 191 for instructions)
- 2 tablespoons Thai fish sauce seasoning
- 1 1/2 tablespoons Thai light soy sauce
- 1 teaspoon ground black pepper
- 2 teaspoons white or brown sugar (optional)
- 1/4 cup vegetable stock or water
- 1/2 cup finely diced red bell pepper
- 1/2 cup finely diced yellow bell pepper
- 1 1/2 tablespoons finely minced lime zest (lime skin)
- 1/2 cup crispy shallots (see page 192 for instructions)
- 1 cup crispy leeks (see page 193 for instructions)

Heat olive oil in a small saucepan over medium heat. Add julienned ginger and stir until it turns crispy or golden brown. Reserving oil, remove crispy ginger with a slotted spoon, drain on paper towels and set aside.

Transfer ginger-infused olive oil into a large skillet over medium high heat. Add garlic and sauté for 30 seconds. Add shrimp, chopped ginger and stir for a minute. Add Jasmine rice, fish sauce, soy sauce, black pepper and sugar, stirring constantly for 2 to 3 minutes. Add vegetable stock, red bell pepper, yellow bell pepper, lime zest and stir for 2 minutes or until ingredients are thoroughly mixed. Transfer ginger fried rice to a serving platter and arrange crispy ginger, shallots and leeks on top.

Enjoy the warm sensation in your mouth. ❖

Green Curry Shrimp Risotto

I often ask myself, what would I like to eat today? Have you ever done that? Of course you have! If you say never, then I know you're lying. Today, once again, I asked myself that question; and I think I'm in a green curry mood. I told you more than once that I prefer my food tasty, not necessarily peppery hot, but tasty. Green curry risotto is very tasty. If you prefer it milder, reduce the amount of green curry paste. If you are a vegetarian, just leave the shrimp in the ocean and you'll still be satisfied.

❖ *Recipe serves 4*

- 2 whole roasted Anaheim chilies
- 3 tablespoons virgin olive oil
- 1 tablespoon chopped fresh garlic
- 1 tablespoon green curry paste
- 1 1/4 cups Thai Jasmine rice
- 1/2 cup white wine
- 6 cups lemongrass stock
- 1 cup sliced bamboo strips
- 2 tablespoons diced Kra-Shy (see page 204)
- 1 can (14 oz.) coconut milk
- 2 tablespoons Thai fish sauce seasoning
- 3 teaspoons honey or sugar
- 20 large shrimp size 13 to 15 per lb.
- 1 cup asparagus sliced into 1 inch lengths
- 1/2 cup Thai basil or regular basil
- *3 tablespoons crispy sliced Kaffir lime leaves
- *1 cup crispy Thai basil leaves for garnish

Place Anaheim chilies on a wire rack over low heat gas burner and grill until blistered on all sides. Transfer roasted Anaheim chilies to a small plastic or paper bag, close bag and let it cool. Peel and seed chilies, dice into small pieces and set aside.

Place olive oil and garlic into a large deep skillet over medium heat and sauté for a minute until light brown. Add green curry paste and stir for a minute or until light green color appears. Add Jasmine rice and stir constantly for 1 to 2 minutes. Add white wine and sauté for 2 to 3 minutes, until wine reduces by half. Add 4 cups of lemongrass stock, bamboo shoots, Kra-Shy and stir constantly for 5 minutes. Add coconut milk, fish sauce and honey and cook for 2 minutes. Add shrimp and asparagus and stir for 2 to 3 minutes. Risotto should be moist and not too dry. Add more lemongrass stock as needed. Remove from heat. Add basil and stir until mixed. Transfer to 4 serving bowls and garnish with crispy Kaffir lime leaves and crispy basil.

* Making crispy Kaffir lime leaves and basil is the same as making crispy leeks. Please turn to page 193 for instructions. ❖

Mango Curry with Sticky Rice

So! If you think mango is for dessert only in Thai cuisine, think again! Mango with sweet sticky rice is a great dessert that all Thais love to eat when it's in season. Mango can be a salad that's called, what else, Mango Salad. You can make mango salsa, mango chutney, jam, mango juice, and tea. Now, what more do you want from mango? Oh yes, Mango Curry...

❖ *Recipe serves 4*

- 3 tablespoons ginger olive oil
- 1/2 cup sliced shallots
- 2 cups chopped ripe mango (select the sweet variety)
- 1/2 cup diced carrots
- 1/2 cup diced red bell pepper
- 2 teaspoons curry powder
- 1 teaspoon sea salt
- 1 cup coconut milk
- 1 cup plain yogurt
- 4 cups cooked sticky rice (white or black rice) (see page 191 for instructions)
- 4 roasted jalapenos sliced 1/2 inch strips
- 1/4 cup water
- 1/3 cup crispy ginger (see page 193 for instructions)
- 1/3 cup crispy shallots (see page 192 for instructions)
- 1 tablespoon black sesame seeds for garnish
- 2 tablespoons finely sliced chives for garnish

Place ginger olive oil and shallots into a deep skillet over medium high heat and stir for 1 minute. Add mango and carrots and stir for 2 to 3 minutes. Add bell pepper, curry powder, salt and coconut milk and bring sauce to a boil. Add yogurt and water, stir and bring sauce to a boil. Reduce heat to low and simmer for 10 minutes, stirring every 2 minutes. Add jalapeno chili and bring sauce to a boil, remove from heat and set aside. Place 1 cup of sticky rice into a round or triangular mold and un-mold on the center of each plate. Place mango curry sauce around the molded rice. Place crispy ginger and shallots on top of rice and garnish with chives and black sesame seeds. ❖

Mistake on The Lake

It's a beautiful day outside; the sun is out to play and is accompanied by a cool breeze. I was going to make smoked sausages with Black Olive Rice for lunch at the boathouse on Lake Erie with the Ruggerio family. I took some sausage and quickly chopped it and the rest of the ingredients we prepped the day before. I have so many green olives on the shelves but no black ones are to be found. Well, if I put in extra sweet black bean sauce, the green may turn black. While we ate the rice, I was thinking to myself, this sausage is spicy but not too smoky, so I went back to the kitchen to look at the package. You already know what it is, I guess... It's a good day on the lake to make a sausage mistake!!!

❖ *Recipe serves 4*

- 3 cups sliced red onions
- 1 tablespoon garlic olive oil (see page 192 for instructions)
- 1 teaspoon sea salt
- 1 tablespoon sugar
- 3 tablespoons finely chopped Italian parsley
- 1/3 cup virgin olive oil
- 4 whole fresh Kee Noo chilies finely chopped (substitute with 2 Serrano chilies)
- 2 tablespoons finely chopped garlic
- 2 cups chopped pepperoni (use a spicy brand)
- 1 cup finely chopped green olives
- 6 cups cooked Basmati rice (see page 191 for instructions)
- 2 teaspoons salt-free Thai seasoning
- 1 1/2 tablespoons sweet black bean sauce
- 1/2 cup vegetable stock or fresh water
- 1/2 cup shredded carrots
- 3/4 cup finely diced red bell peppers
- 1 tablespoon finely sliced fresh Kaffir lime leaves
- 3 tablespoons sliced chives
- 4 olive sprigs or chive flowers for garnish

Place red onions and garlic olive oil into a skillet over medium heat and cook for 8 minutes or until onion is caramelized. Add salt and sugar and stir for a minute. Add parsley and stir until thoroughly mixed. Remove and set aside.

Place olive oil, chili and garlic into a large skillet over high heat and stir for a minute. Add pepperoni and stir for 2 minutes. Add green olives and rice and stir for 3 to 4 minutes. Add remaining ingredients except sliced chives and olive sprigs, and stir constantly for 3 to 4 minutes. Remove to a large platter. Place caramelized onion on top of cooked rice and sprinkle sliced chives around the platter, garnish with olive sprigs or chive flowers.

Learn to enjoy your mistakes... ❖

Grilled Thai Tiger Prawns with Mango Risotto

I used sweet mango to tone down the spiciness of this risotto and it worked. The Royal Thai Government, Export Department, asked me at the last minute to do a cooking demo using Thai Tiger Prawns and other Thai food ingredients. When I was cooking in front of the audience of hundreds, I didn't know what to expect, since I never had a chance to experiment with this dish beforehand. I'm glad it turned out great; otherwise it would never have made it onto this page.

❖ *Recipe serves 4*

- 12 large *Thai tiger prawns. (size 11 to 13 per lb.)
- 2 tablespoons virgin olive oil
- 1 tablespoon salt-free Thai seasoning
- 3 tablespoons virgin olive oil
- 1 tablespoon chopped garlic
- 1 tablespoon panang curry paste
- 1 cup Thai Jasmine rice
- 4 cups lemongrass stock (see page 196)
- 1 can. (14 oz.) coconut milk
- 1/2 cup diced red bell peppers
- 1 cup diced tomatoes
- 2 tablespoons Thai fish sauce seasoning
- 1 teaspoon palm sugar or honey
- 1 1/2 cups mushrooms (oyster, shiitake or enoki)
- 2 whole sweet sun ripened mangos — peeled seeded and cut into bite-size pieces
- 1/2 cup Half & Half
- 1/4 cup ** Cooked Thai black rice (Thai wild rice)
- 2 teaspoons very thinly sliced Kaffir lime leaves
- 1/2 cup Thai or regular basil
- 1/4 cup grated Parmesan cheese (optional)
- 4 sprigs Thai or regular basil for garnish

Place olive oil, garlic and panang curry paste into a large deep skillet over medium high heat and stir for a minute or until red color appears. Add Jasmine rice, stirring constantly for one minute. Add lemongrass stock and cook for 5 minutes, stirring constantly to keep rice from sticking to the bottom of the skillet. Add coconut milk, red bell pepper, tomatoes, fish sauce, palm sugar and cook for 2 minutes. (Meanwhile, heat up a grill for the prawns.) Add mushrooms, mango, half & half and cook for 5 to 7 minutes. While rice is cooking, coat Tiger prawns with olive oil and Thai seasoning and place on a hot grill. Grill the prawns 3 to 4 minutes on each side. Now stirring risotto constantly, add cooked Thai wild rice, Kaffir lime leaves and basil. Remove mango risotto to 4 serving bowls and garnish with basil sprigs. Arrange tiger prawns on top of or around Mango Risotto.

** Cooked Thai wild rice: Place wild rice and 2 cups of fresh water into a small stockpot over high heat and bring to boil. Reduce heat to medium and cook for 15 minutes. Remove, drain, rinse with cold water and set aside. ❖

Spinach Risotto

P**opeye said if you want to be strong, have a bunch of spinach. Well, eating spinach by itself is not my cup of tea, unless it is accompanied with a great vinaigrette. Oh yeah! You can try Lemongrass vinaigrette or you can make this recipe. I think you'll enjoy it tremendously. Please make sure the risotto is not too dry, it should still be moist and the rice still* ***al dente *(slightly firm).*

❖ *Recipe serves 4*

- 8 cups water
- 1 teaspoon sea salt
- 2 bunches spinach rinsed with stems removed (yields 2 cups blanched spinach)
- 4 tablespoons virgin olive oil
- 4 tablespoons finely minced shallots
- $1\frac{1}{4}$ cup Thai Jasmine rice
- 1 tablespoon finely minced Serrano chilies
- 2 teaspoons white pepper
- 1 cup white wine
- 7 cups lemongrass stock (see page196)
- 1 cup seeded diced Roma tomatoes
- $1\frac{1}{2}$ cups shiitake mushrooms cut into small strips
- 1 cup milk
- 2 tablespoons Thai fish sauce seasoning
- 4 tablespoons freshly grated Parmesan cheese (optional)

Bring water and salt to a boil in a stockpot over high heat. Add spinach and push it down with a spatula until spinach wilts. Drain and squeeze excess liquid and set aside.

Heat virgin olive oil in a deep heavy skillet over medium high heat. Add shallots and sauté for a minute. Add Jasmine rice and sauté for a minute. Add Serrano chilies and white pepper and sauté for a minute. Add white wine and bring rice to a boil, about 3 to 4 minutes. Add 3 cups of lemongrass stock and stir constantly for 4 minutes and reduce heat to medium low. Add tomatoes, mushrooms, blanched spinach, milk and fish sauce seasonings, stirring constantly for 6 to 7 minutes. While you are stirring, add lemongrass stock as needed. Remove spinach risotto from heat and transfer to serving bowl. Sprinkle with Parmesan cheese if you prefer and serve at once. ❖

T.F.R

***W**hy do we call it T.F.R.? Now let me tell you why. I travel a lot, both my kids can second that! One day I returned home from a trip and I went to my restaurant to have dinner. I always make a point to stop by the restaurant after a trip. The restaurant was very busy, and it happened to be a week that one of our chefs was under the weather. I went in the kitchen to give them a hand. "Yes! Of course I still can cook." I answered one of our kitchen associates when he jokingly asked me: "can you still cook?" They gave me my usual position on the line and I tried to keep up with the orders that were bombarding me. When my expediter called, "T.F.R", I barked back, "What the hell is that?" Well, they said calling out Tommy Fried Rice takes too long so we changed it to T.F.R. I was dumbfounded, but the name stayed.*

❖ *Recipe serves 4*

Caramelized beef

- 2 tablespoons olive oil
- 2 tablespoons finely chopped garlic
- 12 oz. sliced filet of beef $\frac{1}{4}$ inch by 2 inch strips
- $1\frac{1}{2}$ tablespoons sugar or honey
- 1 tablespoon finely chopped, peeled fresh ginger
- 2 teaspoons ground black pepper
- $\frac{3}{4}$ cup coconut milk
- $1\frac{1}{2}$ tablespoons Thai fish sauce seasoning
- $1\frac{1}{2}$ tablespoons sweet black bean sauce
- $\frac{3}{4}$ cup sliced brown onions
- 3 dried Kee Noo chilies

Rice

- 4 tablespoons olive or vegetable oil
- 12 oz. chicken breast cut into small strips
- 2 fresh eggs
- 1 cup sliced brown onions
- 3 tablespoons oyster sauce
- 2 tablespoons Thai fish sauce seasoning
- 2 tablespoons light soy sauce
- 2 teaspoons sweet black bean sauce
- 6 cups cooked Jasmine rice
- 1 teaspoon ground white pepper
- $\frac{3}{4}$ cup small diced tomatoes
- $\frac{1}{4}$ cup finely sliced scallions
- $\frac{1}{4}$ cup sliced cilantro leaves

Place olive oil, garlic and beef into a skillet over medium heat and cook for 3 to 4 minutes. Add sugar, ginger, black pepper and stir for 1 minute. Add remaining ingredients and bring to a boil. Reduce heat to low and simmer for 17 to 20 minutes or until sauce becomes thick. Remove and set aside.

While beef simmers, place oil and chicken into a large frying pan over medium high heat and stir for 2 to 3 minutes, until chicken is half cooked. Strike 2 eggs into the skillet and let cook for a minute before stirring them. Add brown onions, oyster sauce, fish sauce, soy sauce, black bean sauce and stir for a minute. Add rice and white pepper and stir constantly for 3 minutes. Add tomatoes and stir for 2 to 3 minutes. Remove from heat and transfer to serving platter. Place caramelized beef on top of cooked rice and sprinkle with scallions and cilantro. ❖

Texas Fried Rice

You know what 1015 means? Let me tell you about it. I went to Houston, Texas to teach a cooking class and when I told my class brown onions; they corrected me by saying 1015. I said 1015? What is 1015? They said, that's what we locals call brown onions. You know who you are, cowboys/girls, if you happen to get this book!

❖ *Recipe serves 4*

$^{1}/_{4}$ cup olive or vegetable oil	1 cup brown onions
$1^{1}/_{2}$ tablespoons finely chopped garlic	2 cups finely diced tomatoes
2 cups cooked crayfish (meat only)	$^{1}/_{4}$ cup seracha chili pepper sauce
6 cups cooked Thai Jasmine rice	4 tablespoons Thai fish sauce seasoning
$^{1}/_{4}$ cup finely diced carrots	$1^{1}/_{2}$ tablespoons salt-free Thai seasoning
$^{1}/_{4}$ cup corn kernels	$^{1}/_{2}$ cup finely sliced scallions (garnish)
$^{1}/_{4}$ cup sweet peas	$^{1}/_{3}$ cup sliced cilantro leaves (garnish)

Place olive oil into a large skillet over high heat. Add garlic and stir for $1^{1}/_{2}$ minutes. Add crayfish (substitute with shrimp) and rice and stir for a minute. Add remaining ingredients except garnish ingredients. Stir constantly for 3-4 minutes until ingredients mix thoroughly. Add $^{1}/_{3}$-cup water, if rice is a little bit dry. Transfer Texas Fried Rice to a large bowl and garnish with scallions and cilantro. ❖

Thai Herbs Sausage Risotto

When you think sausage, you probably think pork, but not I. I think sausage can be made from different meats, poultry, seafood and even vegetables. You can mix these sausage recipe ingredients and stuff into a casing but if you don't like the casing, you can use a sheet of plastic wrap and roll them like sushi rolls. Then you steam the sausage links. That's how we do the (housemade) sausage in my restaurant. Of course they have to be grilled or seared before you serve them. You can use my combination, chicken and shrimp, or you can do it your own way.

❖ *Recipe serves 4*

Herb sausage

- 8 large shrimp shelled and deveined
- 8 oz. minced chicken breast
- 1/2 teaspoon salt-free Thai seasoning
- 2 teaspoons Thai fish sauce seasoning
- 1 tablespoon finely chopped tender lemongrass
- 1 teaspoon finely minced Kaffir lime leaves

Rice & Sauce

- 3 tablespoons virgin olive oil
- 1 tablespoon chopped garlic
- 1 tablespoon Thai panang or red curry paste
- 1 1/4 cups Thai Jasmine rice (about 9 oz.)
- 4 cups lemongrass stock (see page 196)
- 1-14 oz. can. coconut milk
- 2 tablespoons Thai fish sauce seasoning
- 1 teaspoon palm sugar or honey
- 1/2 cup diced red bell peppers
- 1 cup diced seeded tomatoes
- 1/2 cup half & half
- 2 teaspoons thinly sliced Kaffir lime leaves
- 1/2 cup Thai or regular basil
- 1/4 cup thinly sliced scallions
- 1/4 cup grated Parmesan cheese
- 4 sprigs Thai or regular basil for garnish

Combine Thai herb sausage ingredients in a small bowl, mix thoroughly and set aside.

Place olive oil, garlic, and red curry paste into a large deep skillet over medium high heat and sauté for a minute or two, until red color from curry paste appears. Add Jasmine rice, stirring constantly for a minute. Add 3 cups lemongrass stock, and cook for 4 to 5 minutes, stirring constantly to keep rice from sticking to the bottom of the skillet.

Add Thai herb sausage mixture, a small amount at a time and stir for 2 minutes. Add coconut milk, fish sauce, palm sugar, red bell pepper, tomatoes, and cook for 3 to 4 minutes, stirring constantly. Add half & half and stir constantly for 2 to 3 minutes. If risotto is to dry, add remaining lemongrass stock as needed. Add Kaffir lime leaves and basil; stir until thoroughly blended. Remove risotto to 4 serving bowls and sprinkle with scallions, grated Parmesan cheese, and garnish with basil sprigs.❖

Wild Mushroom Risotto

When I made this dish in the 80's everybody got what I was doing with the risotto. My Italian friends asked me, are you going to cook Italian food? I told them absolutely not, I made rice soup, a thicker version of Asian rice soup that you can get anywhere in Thailand or China. Italy just made it famous and easier and called it risotto rather than thick rice soup, don't you think?

❖ *Recipe serves 4*

- 3 tablespoons virgin olive oil
- 1 can coconut milk (13.5 to 14 oz.)
- 1 tablespoon chopped garlic
- 2 cups mixed wild mushrooms such as oyster, shiitake, portobello and chanterelle
- 1 tablespoon Panang curry paste
- 2 tablespoons Thai fish sauce seasoning
- 1 1/4 cups Thai Jasmine rice (about 9 oz.)
- 1 teaspoon honey or sugar
- 4 cups lemongrass stock (see page 196 for instructions)
- 1/2 cup half & half or milk
- 1/2 cup diced red bell peppers
- 1/4 cup pan roasted pine nuts
- 2 cups diced tomatoes
- 1/4 cup minced Italian parsley leaves
- 1/4 cup finely diced sun-dried tomatoes soaked in water and drained
- 1/2 cup grated Parmesan cheese (optional)

Place olive oil, panang curry paste, and garlic into a large deep skillet over medium high heat and stir for a minute or until red color appeared. Add rice and stir constantly for one minute. Add lemongrass stock, and cook for 5 to 6 minutes, stir every minute to keep rice from sticking to bottom of skillet. Add red bell peppers, tomatoes, sun dried tomatoes and stir for a minute. Add coconut milk, mushrooms, fish sauce, honey and stir constantly for 4 minutes. Add half & half, pine nuts and stir until thoroughly mixed. Remove Thai Risotto to 4 serving bowls and sprinkle with parsley and Parmesan cheese if desired. ❖

● Have wagon with travel.

Bangkok @ night.

PASTA

City of Angels

Touring Thailand was nothing like I had ever seen nor expected. As I got off that luxurious Thai Airways, and stepped into this new environment, not to mention intense humidity, I felt a strange vibe. At first my intentions were to whine as much as possible until I got to get back on that plane with the nice air conditioning, but when I saw the smiles of the Thai people so excited that new Americans were here to visit their home, I couldn't back out. I tried to smile back, but the heat seemed to intensify each step I took. Walking through the airport in this city I knew nothing about Bangkok, I started to eye a few things on the wall, and I came across maps, and pictures of what I soon learned was a city of Angels, "not LA". I gradually became interested and anxious to step beyond airport territory into this new adventurous place. After we received our luggage, and went through customs, we were ready to set out on this mysterious adventure. As I stepped on our big tour bus, I quickly took my own personal seat near the window. This place was completely different from LA. People made a living selling fresh fruit on a sidewalk or in an alley. It was amazing, and although many people may see that as a low class job, these workers were some of the happiest people I've ever seen. When we walked into the hotel, we had yet another warm welcome, this time it included juices of Thailand.

After a few days of eating the Thai fruits and foods, meeting the Thai people, and seeing their overall culture, I soon began to fall in love with this city. So many people lived there, and although the economy is not like it is in America, people there seem to be so content with their lives, and much more appreciative than many people I know. It was definitely an experience that I could never forget. The warmth of Thailand filled me with a strange feeling that I long for whenever I'm not there. This was one trip I could never forget.

Aisha Tang

Bowtie Pasta with Mushrooms and Caramelized Red Onion

This pasta is very easy to cook; it doesn't take long and is very satisfying. I used to go on the road to demonstrate how to use Tommy Tang's seasonings and sauces. When I did a demonstration at Tops supermarket in Buffalo, New York, I was doing T.F.R. sauce and someone asked me, can this sauce go with pasta? I said of course, this sauce can be used for everything! My wife Sandi used to say this sauce made shoe leather taste good! I just wonder if she really tried it! And yes, I did show the lady how to make this pasta using T.F.R. sauce but in case you can't find one in your neck of the woods, this is the recipe. If you have read this book, you will know what T.F.R. means, if you still don't know, it's time to read the book over again.

❖ *Recipe serves 4*

- 2 cups bowtie pasta
- 10 cups water
- 1/2 teaspoon salt
- 1/4 cup olive oil
- 2 cups sliced red onions
- 1 tablespoon chopped garlic
- 4 cups sliced mushrooms
- 2 cups diced tomatoes
- 1 cup thinly sliced red or yellow bell pepper
- 1 tablespoon roasted sesame oil
- 1 1/2 tablespoons Thai fish sauce seasoning
- 2 tablespoons oyster sauce
- 1 tablespoon sweet black bean sauce
- 1 cup vegetable stock or fresh water
- 2 tablespoons ground black pepper
- 2 tablespoons finely chopped Italian parsley
- 1/2 cup finely sliced scallions
- 1/4 cup shaved Parmesan cheese (optional)
- 2 teaspoons Kee Noo chili flakes (optional)

Place water into a large stockpot over high heat and bring to a boil. Add pasta, olive oil and salt and cook for 10-12 minutes. Drain and rinse pasta with cold water and set aside.

Place 1 tablespoon olive oil and red onions into a medium skillet over medium heat and sauté for 10-12 minutes or until it caramelizes and set aside.

Place remaining olive oil and garlic into a large deep skillet over medium high heat and sauté for 1 minute. Add mushrooms and stir for 4 to 5 minutes. Add tomatoes, red bell pepper, sesame oil, fish sauce, oyster sauce, sweet black bean sauce and stir for 2 minutes. Add vegetable stock, black pepper and bring sauce to a boil. Add pasta and stir for 3-4 minutes. Remove pasta to a serving bowl and add caramelized red onions on top. Sprinkle with parsley, scallions and cheese. ❖

Osso Buco with Thai Curry Pasta

I love very tender Osso Buco, (veal shank) which I always enjoyed when I lived in New York City. Did I tell you? I used to have a restaurant in Tribeca NYC, in 1986. Of course, I no longer have it, that's why I said I used to. Tribeca means "Triangle Below Canal Street," get it? My restaurant was located on Greenwich Street and was not far to walk to Chinatown and Little Italy. Since there are so many great restaurants in Little Italy, I often walked over to have some great Italian food like Osso Buco. I made this dish as a special when we had enough time to cook in the kitchen. I thought to myself, one day I will put this recipe in my cookbook, and here you have it.

❖ *Recipe serves 4*

Marinade

- 4 pieces large veal shank
- 2 tablespoons virgin olive oil
- 10 cloves finely chopped garlic
- $^{1}/_{4}$ cup sliced lemongrass
- 2 tablespoons finely minced Kaffir lime leaves
- 1 tablespoon cracked black pepper
- 1 teaspoon sea salt
- 2 tablespoons virgin olive oil (for seared veal shank)
- 2 cups chicken or vegetable stock

Thai curry

- 2 tablespoons virgin olive oil
- 1 tablespoon panang curry paste
- 2 teaspoons chopped fresh garlic
- 2 tablespoons chopped shallots
- 1 tablespoon finely chopped fresh ginger
- 1 cup red wine
- $^{1}/_{4}$ cup sun-dried tomatoes soaked in water and drained
- $^{1}/_{2}$ cup diced red bell pepper
- 1 can (14 oz.) coconut milk
- 4 cups lemon grass or vegetable stock
- 2 teaspoons honey or raw sugar
- 2 teaspoons sea salt
- 1 cup half & half
- 1 cup yellow or red cherry tomatoes cut in half
- 1 teaspoon finely minced Kaffir lime leaves
- $^{1}/_{2}$ cup Thai basil
- 10 cups boiling water
- 12 oz. angel hair pasta

Combine olive oil, garlic, lemongrass, Kaffir lime leaves, black pepper and sea salt in a large mixing bowl. Add veal shanks and rub until thoroughly coated and set aside in refrigerator for 2 hours.

Place 2 tablespoons olive oil in a large oven-proof skillet over high heat. Add veal shank and sear 3 minutes each side. Add lemongrass stock and transfer seared veal shanks to a preheated oven at 400° F. and cook for 30 minutes. Baste veal shank every 5 minutes with liquid that is in the skillet. Remove veal shank to a plate, let it rest and set aside.

Place olive oil, panang, garlic, shallots and ginger into a deep saucepan over medium heat and stir for 2 minutes. Add red wine and cook until reduced by half, remove and set aside.

Place a half can of coconut milk into a blender and stir, add cooked curry mixture, sun dried tomatoes and red bell pepper to blender and blend until smooth and transfer to the same deep sauce pan. Add remaining coconut milk, lemongrass stock, honey, and sea salt and bring sauce to a boil. Add veal shanks, reduce heat to lowest temperature and simmer for 45 minutes. Add half & half, cherry tomatoes, Kaffir lime leaves and bring sauce to a boil. Reduce heat to low and simmer for 10 to 15 minutes.

While veal shanks are being simmered, place pasta into boiling water and cook for 2 minutes. Remove and drain pasta in a colander. Transfer cooked veal shanks to a serving plate and bring sauce to boil. Add cooked pasta to the sauce stirring constantly for 1 to 2 minutes. Add basil and toss until thoroughly mixed. Remove pasta and place around veal shanks. ❖

Buffalo Wing Noodles

One afternoon, while writing this book in Buffalo, New York, guess what I ordered for lunch? Buffalo wings, that's right. After all, this is the birthplace of Buffalo wings. When I first heard about Buffalo wings, I thought this town had nothing better to do than turn Buffalos into Angels. You see, when I saw movies, anything that had wings was an Angel! But this Angel has only wings and is a chicken no less, not even Buffalo. Soooo Des Garr in Japanese means "Is that right? " Yes! That's right, chicken wings in Buffalo are called Buffalo Wings. Now what does all this mumble jumble have to do with this recipe? I had leftover Buffalo wings from my lunch and I'm not gonna throw them away. Rather, I made up this recipe for you.

Have wings will fly! But I ain't no Angel; I'm just chicken wings on top of noodles.

❖ *Recipe serves 4*

- 24 pieces chicken wings cut in half and discard tips
- 1/3 cup red wine
- 2 tablespoons salt-free Thai seasoning
- 2 teaspoons sea salt
- 10 oz. linguine pasta or soft Mee Krob noodles
- 8 cups water
- 1/2 teaspoon sea salt
- 2 tablespoons virgin olive oil
- 1 tablespoon chopped garlic
- 1/4 cup sliced shallots
- 1/2 cup Seracha chili pepper sauce
- 1/2 cup white wine
- 2 cups reserved pasta liquid
- 1 1/2 cups diced, seeded tomatoes
- 1/2 cup shredded carrots
- 1 cup sliced brown onions
- 1 cup thinly sliced white cap mushrooms
- 2 tablespoons Thai fish sauce seasoning
- 2 teaspoons sugar
- 1/2 cup thin sliced scallions
- 3 tablespoons chopped parsley

Recipe continue next page ▸

Combine wings, red wine, seasoning and salt into a mixing bowl to marinade for 1 hour. Place marinated wings into a preheated oven at 400°F. and bake for 30 minutes, turning every 10 minutes. Turn off oven and let baked wings stay warm in the oven.

While wings are in the oven, combine water and salt into a large stockpot over high heat and bring to boil. Add linguine pasta and cook for 9 minutes, drain and set aside. (Reserve 2 cups of pasta liquid for sauce)

Place olive oil, garlic and shallots into a deep skillet over high heat and sauté for a minute. Add Seracha chili pepper sauce, white wine, baked chicken wings and $^1/_4$ cup pasta-cooking liquid and stir for 2 minutes. Reduce heat to medium and cover with a lid and cook for 4-5 minutes. Remove wings (without sauce) and place in a bowl and put into oven to keep warm. Add tomatoes, carrots and onions into sauce and bring to a boil. Add mushrooms, fish sauce and sugar, stir for 1 minute and add remaining pasta liquid and bring sauce to a boil. Reduce heat to medium low and simmer for 3-4 minutes. Add cooked pasta and stir constantly until pasta is thoroughly coated. Remove pasta to a large platter and arrange Buffalo wings around pasta. Sprinkle with scallions and parsley. ❖

• Thai water buffalo.

Nam Prik Noom Pasta (Young Chili Sauce Pasta)

The heat from the sauce is so intense that sweat is running down my face, like an open faucet that broke. Sweating so much on your head keeps you young, I guess.

❖ *Serves 4*

- 8 whole Serrano chilies (for lower heat use less chilies)
- 2 whole Anaheim chilies
- 6 large shallots with skin on
- 8 cloves large garlic with skin on
- 6 whole medium size Roma tomatoes
- 1 1/2 teaspoons sea salt
- 1 tablespoon Thai fish sauce seasoning
- 2 tablespoons fresh lime or lemon juice
- 12 oz. spaghetti
- 8 cups water
- 1 teaspoon sea salt

Wrap Serrano and Anaheim chilies, shallots, and garlic in aluminum foil. Wrap them tightly. Wrap tomatoes in a separate sheet of aluminum foil and place both on a grill or on a wire rack over low heat on an open flame burner. Grill them until blistered, remove and put into a bowl, cover with a lid or a zip-lock plastic bag and allow them to cool so skins can be easily peeled. With a small knife, peel all grilled ingredients and put into a food processor, add sea salt, coarsely chop and transfer to a mixing bowl. Add fish sauce and lime juice, mix thoroughly and set aside. Bring water and salt to a boil in a medium stockpot over high heat. Add pasta and cook for 10-11 minutes. Drain and transfer to a large bowl and pour cold Nam Prik Noom over hot pasta. Serve pasta immediately.

Have a healthy sweat!!!

• **Come see me in Chiang Rai.**

Black Pasta with Roasted Garlic Sun Dried Tomato Sauce

If you've never cooked with sun dried tomatoes before, they come in different varieties. Please make sure to use the one with less salt or without salt. If you like to dry them yourself, core and cut tomatoes in half and lay on a large baking tray in the sun. It will take 3 to 4 days (in Thailand, a full day sun drying, we call them one sun) depending on how hot the sun is in your area.

❖ *Recipe serves 4*

10 pieces sun dried tomatoes soaked in 2 cups of water	1/3 cup white wine
12 cloves garlic skins intact	1 1/2 tablespoons Thai fish sauce seasoning
8 whole shallots skins intact	3 tablespoons finely chopped parsley
3 whole red bell pepper	12 oz. black pasta (spaghetti or linguine)
1/2 teaspoon sea salt	8 cups water
3 tablespoons virgin olive oil	1/2 teaspoon sea salt

Soak sun dried tomatoes in 2 cups of water for 1 hour. Separately wrap garlic and shallots in aluminum foil and fold to cover (2-3 folds). Squeeze to make the packets airtight. Place wrapped garlic, shallots, and red bell pepper onto a preheated grill or onto a burner with a wire rack over medium low heat. Grill garlic and shallots for 6-7 minutes. (Red bell pepper for 9-10 minutes). Place grilled ingredients into a bowl and cover with plastic wrap. Allow them to sweat, to facilitate the removal of the skins. Place skinned garlic and shallots into a food processor and chop coarsely, remove and set aside. Place skinned and seeded red bell peppers, drained sun dried tomatoes, (reserve sun dried tomato water for making sauce) and salt into the same food processor and puree, remove and set aside.

Place olive oil, and chopped garlic and shallots into a large skillet over high heat and sauté for 2 minutes. Add white wine and sauté for 3-4 minutes. Add sun dried tomatoes, red bell pepper puree, and fish sauce, stir and bring sauce to a boil. Add reserved water and bring sauce to a boil. Reduce heat to medium low and simmer for 7 to 8 minutes.

While sauce is simmering, place water and salt into a stockpot over high heat and bring to a boil. Add pasta and cook for 9 to10 minutes, drain and transfer pasta to roasted garlic sauce and mix until pasta is thoroughly coated. Add chopped parsley and stir into pasta, transfer to a platter and serve. ❖

Linguine Pasta with Green Curry Beef Sauce

One winter night in Los Angeles, I stayed home alone with my wife Sandi, which is very rare, because we have two daughters. But tonight, they had both gone to sleep over at their friend's house. We were alone at last. We planned to have dinner and later see a movie. But man, it is cold outside tonight; the fire is still on and it feels so warm and cozy. Why go out? she said, Let's stay home and order delivery. I told her I had green curry beef in the fridge and I could cook some Thai Jasmine rice to go with it. I warmed up the green curry, she looks at it and I know she prefers her curry a little thicker and creamier. While back at the fire in the living room, I added sour cream and voila... the curry is much thicker, the way my wife likes it. I had to make linguine pasta instead of rice and you know why? Because she wants it and it beats going out on a freezing cold night!

❖ *Recipe serves 4*

- 12 oz. linguine pasta
- 8 cups water
- 1 teaspoon sea salt
- 3 tablespoons olive oil
- 1 tablespoon finely chopped garlic
- 1 tablespoon green curry paste
- 1 can (14 oz.) coconut milk
- 1 1/2 cups sliced filet of beef strips
- 1 1/2 cups sliced bamboo shoots
- 1 tablespoon palm sugar
- 2 tablespoons Thai fish sauce seasoning
- 1 cup water
- 1/2 cup thinly sliced Thai green eggplant
- 1/2 cup thinly sliced red bell pepper
- 1/2 cup carrots half inch diced
- 1/4 cup sliced Jalapeno chili strips
- 2 tablespoons sliced Kaffir lime leaves
- 1/2 cup sour cream
- 1 cup Thai basil leaves

Place water into a stockpot over high heat and bring to a boil. Add pasta and salt and cook for 9 -10 minutes, drain and rinse in cold water and set aside.

While pasta is cooking, heat olive oil in a skillet over medium high heat. Add garlic and green curry paste and stir for 2 minutes. Add 1/4 cup coconut milk and stir for a minute. Add beef, bamboo shoots and remaining coconut milk and bring sauce to a boil. Add palm sugar, fish sauce, water and bring sauce to a boil. Add Thai green eggplants, red bell pepper, carrots and jalapeno, Kaffir lime leaves and bring sauce to a boil. Reduce heat to medium low and simmer for 15-20 minutes. Add sour cream and bring sauce to a boil. Add cooked pasta, and stir until pasta is thoroughly coated. Transfer pasta to a large bowl and sprinkle Thai basil over pasta. If you would like some good Parmesan cheese, go right ahead. I prefer this without.❖

Perciatelli Pasta with Malaysian Clams and Thai Basil Sauce

The first time I had linguine with clam sauce was at a restaurant in Blythe, California. Blythe is located on the border next to Arizona. If you are driving on Interstate 10 eastward, Blythe is the last city just before you cross the bridge over the Colorado River. The restaurant serves it only with red clam sauce. I like mine with white clam sauce and they don't serve it with Malaysian clams, just ordinary chopped clams, probably clams packed in a can or jar. Anyway I loved it, and since then I have had a chance to taste linguine with white clam sauce from many great restaurants around the country. When I started to fool around with this recipe, I liked it better with Perciatelli pasta. It has a better texture and I even like it this time with fresh tomatoes.

❖ *Recipe for 4*

- 12 oz. Perciatelli pasta
- 10 cups water
- 1/2 teaspoon sea salt
- 4 cups lemongrass stock (see page 196 for instructions)
- 4 lb. Malaysian clams (Manila clams)
- 1/4 cup virgin olive oil
- 2 tablespoons finely chopped garlic
- 1 1/2 tablespoons Thai roasted chili paste
- 2 teaspoons finely chopped fresh Kee Noo chilies
- 1 cup diced brown onions
- 1 cup white wine
- 3/4 cup sliced red bell pepper
- 1 cup diced seeded tomatoes
- 1 cup tomato purée
- 2 cups lemongrass clam broth (from steamed clams)
- 1 tablespoon light soy sauce
- 2 tablespoons Thai fish sauce seasoning
- 1 cup Thai basil
- 4 sprigs Thai basil for garnish

Place water into a stockpot over high heat and bring to a boil. Add pasta and salt and cook for 10 minutes, drain and set aside. Place lemongrass stock into a small stockpot over high heat and bring to a boil. Add clams and cook until they just open. Remove clams from stockpot and remove 2/3 of the cooked clam meat and save 1/3 of cooked clams in the shells for garnish and set aside. Reserve lemongrass and clam broth for making sauce.

Place olive oil and garlic into a deep skillet over medium high heat and sauté for a minute. Add roasted chili paste, Kee Noo chili, onions and sauté for a minute. Add white wine and bring sauce to a boil and cook until sauce reduces by half. Add bell pepper and tomatoes and stir for 2 minutes. Add tomato puree, lemongrass clam broth, light soy sauce, fish sauce and bring to a boil. Reduce heat to low and simmer for 10 minutes. Add cooked pasta and Thai basil, stirring constantly for 2 to 3 minutes. Coat pasta thoroughly with sauce. Remove to pasta serving bowls, arrange reserved cooked clams around the bowls and garnish with Thai basil sprigs. ❖

Sesame Pepper Pasta

This is more or less like stir fried noodles. It doesn't have a lot of sauce but it has lots of flavors. The sesame oil, ginger and chili, create a wonderful sensation in every bite. You can serve this either hot or cold, with or without shrimp and if you prefer it milder, then forget about jalapeno and chili flakes and it will still taste good!

❖ *Recipe serves 4*

- 12 oz. linguine or penne pasta
- 10 cups water
- 1/2 teaspoon sea salt
- 3 tablespoons roasted sesame oil
- 2 tablespoons virgin olive oil
- 1 tablespoon finely chopped garlic
- 1 lb. medium shrimp shelled and deveined
- 1 tablespoon thinly julienned sliced ginger
- 1 cup red bell pepper, thin and long sliced
- 1 cup thinly sliced jalapeno chilies
- 1 cup thinly julienned carrots
- 2 tablespoons fish sauce seasoning
- 2 tablespoons Thai light soy sauce
- 1/4 cup white wine
- 2 teaspoons sugar or honey
- 1 teaspoon ground black pepper
- 1 teaspoon dried chili pepper flakes (optional)
- 1/3 cup sliced chives for garnish

Place water into a stockpot over high heat and bring to a boil. Add pasta and cook for 9-10 minutes, strain and rinse in cold water. Transfer cooked pasta to a mixing bowl. Add sesame oil and coat pasta thoroughly and set aside.

Heat olive oil in a large skillet over medium heat. Add garlic and stir for a minute. Add shrimp, ginger and stir for 3-4 minutes. Add cooked pasta and stir for a minute. Add white wine, fish sauce, soy sauce, sugar, black pepper, chili pepper flakes, and stir constantly for 2 minutes. Remove and transfer to a large pasta bowl. Place red and yellow bell peppers, Jalapeno chilies and carrots on top of pasta and garnish with chives. ❖

● Sunset @ Samui Island.

Shrimp Macaroni

Yes! You read it right, ketchup is in the recipe! Many, many moons ago, someone I knew ordered this dish for me in a coffee shop in Bangkok. It was the first time in my life I ever had such a wonderful dish! I still have fond memories of that day. When I came to the U.S. in the' 70s, I made this dish for a party in my house in Glendale. Everybody liked it and I think it is eatable. You have to understand that most Thai people love this dish. I didn't even know then that macaroni came in different shapes and sizes. Now I know better because of what I do for a living and I must thank the person who introduced this macaroni to me. I can't remember who that person is, but thank you!!

❖ *Recipe serves 4*

- 12 oz. elbow pasta
- $^1/_2$ teaspoon sea salt
- 8 cups fresh water
- 4 tablespoons virgin olive oil
- 1 tablespoon finely chopped garlic
- 1 lb. shrimp shelled and deveined (size 21- 25 per lb.)
- 1 cup diced celery
- 1 cup sliced red bell pepper
- $1^1/_2$ cups sliced brown onions
- $1^1/_2$ cups diced tomatoes
- 2 large eggs
- 4 tablespoons ketchup (substitute with tomato paste)
- 3 tablespoons Thai fish sauce seasoning
- $^1/_2$ cup diced scallions
- 2 teaspoons ground white pepper
- $^1/_2$ cup celery leaves for garnish
- 1 teaspoon Kee Noo chili flakes (optional)

Place water into a stockpot over high heat and bring to a boil. Add macaroni and salt and cook for 10-12 minutes, drain and set aside.

Place virgin olive oil and garlic into a large skillet over medium high heat and sauté for 1 minute or until lightly browned. Add shrimp and stir for 2-3 minutes. Add cooked pasta, celery, bell pepper, brown onions and tomatoes and stir constantly for 3 minutes. Add eggs, ketchup; fish sauce and stir for another 4-5 minutes. Remove and transfer to a serving platter and sprinkle with scallions, white pepper and celery leaves on top, adding Kee Noo chili flakes if desired. ❖

Ziti with Smoked Sausage

This is a good recipe for you when you have a hot dog and sausage BBQ weekend and have lots of leftovers. It is very simple and easy to prepare and if you have anything else in the fridge that you would like to get rid of but don't want to waste, throw it in too! This recipe is definitely for you.

❖ *Serves 4*

- 8 cups water
- 12 oz. spaghetti pasta or other pasta
- ½ teaspoon sea salt
- 3 tablespoons virgin olive oil
- 4 links sliced ¼ inch thick smoked sausage (7-8 inches in length, use the sausage that you prefer)
- 2 tablespoons finely chopped garlic
- 1 cup red wine
- 2 cups sliced red onions
- 1½ cups sliced red bell pepper
- 4 whole jalapeno chilies, seeded, sliced into ¼ inch strips
- 1½ tablespoons Thai fish sauce seasoning
- 2½ cups pasta water
- 2 teaspoons cracked black pepper
- 3 tablespoons finely sliced Italian parsley
- 1 cup sliced leeks, 2 inches in length
- 2 teaspoons dried Thai chili pepper flakes
- ½ cup grated aged Asiago cheese

Bring water and salt to a boil in a large stockpot over high heat. Add pasta and stir occasionally to prevent pasta from sticking to the pot, and boil for 9-10 minutes. Drain and reserve 2½ cups of pasta water for making sauce, and set aside.

While pasta is cooking, place 1 tablespoon of olive oil into a large deep skillet over medium heat. Add smoked sausage and stir occasionally for 2-3 minutes. Add remaining olive oil and garlic and stir for 1-2 minutes or until garlic turns lightly golden brown. Add wine, onions, red bell pepper and jalapeno chilies. Stir until wine sauce is reduced by half. Add pasta water, fish sauce and black pepper. Stir for 2 minutes. Reduce heat to medium low and simmer the sauce for 3 minutes. Add cooked pasta, leeks and parsley and mix it thoroughly. Transfer pasta to a serving bowl, sprinkle with cheese, and add chili flakes if you really like it spicier. ❖

• I'm making kha-nom-kroak (coconut, rice pudding).

Tri Pepper Pasta with Roasted Chili Sauce

This is the same chili paste that is used to make "Hot & Sour Soup" and coconut milk soup, "Tom Kha Kai" I use this chili paste as a sandwich spread or in fried rice. If you combine with lime juice and fish sauce, you've just made a "roasted chili dipping sauce."

❖ *Recipe serves 4*

- 12 oz. linguine pasta
- 8 cups water
- 1 teaspoon sea salt
- 3 tablespoons virgin olive oil
- 1 1/2 tablespoons finely chopped garlic
- 1 tablespoon Thai roasted chili paste
- 3/4 cup red wine
- 1 cup red bell pepper purée (see page 197 for instructions)
- 1 1/2 cups diced tomatoes
- 1/2 tablespoon palm sugar or honey
- 2 tablespoons Thai fish sauce seasoning
- 1/2 cup thinly sliced red bell pepper
- 1/2 cup thinly sliced yellow bell pepper
- 1/4 cup thinly sliced jalapeno chilies
- 1 cup thai basil leaves
- 1/3 cup fresh grated Parmesan cheese (optional)

Place water into a stockpot over high heat and bring to a boil. Add pasta and salt and cook for 10 - 11 minutes, drain, rinse in cold water and set aside.

While pasta is cooking, heat olive oil in a large skillet over medium high heat. Add garlic and roasted chili paste and sauté for 2 minutes. Add red wine and sauté for 3 to 4 minutes or until sauce reduces by half. Add red bell pepper purée, tomatoes, palm sugar, fish sauce and bring sauce to a boil. Reduce to medium low and simmer for 8 minutes. Add cooked pasta, and stir for 2 minutes until pasta is thoroughly coated. Transfer pasta to a large bowl and toss red and yellow bell pepper and jalapeno on top. Garnish with Thai basil. Sprinkle with Parmesan cheese if desired. ❖

Spicy Penne with Roasted Bell Pepper

***B**e prepared! If you are making this pasta, it is* **very** *spicy. When you add Kee Noo chili flakes into hot oil, the heat from the chili will explode in the air and if you inhale the fumes, you're certain to have a good cough. CAUTION: Please make sure that no small children are around the kitchen when you prepare this dish!!*

❖ *Recipe serves 4*

- 8 cups water
- 1 tablespoon olive or vegetable oil
- 1/2 teaspoon salt
- 12 oz. penne pasta
- 1 whole roasted and julienned red bell pepper
- 1 whole roasted and julienned yellow or golden bell pepper
- 1/4 cup virgin olive oil
- 10 cloves garlic sliced
- 1 tablespoon dried crushed Kee Noo chili flakes
- 1/4 cup white wine (optional)
- 1 1/2 cups diced Roma tomatoes
- 1 cup lemongrass or vegetable stock (see page 196 for instructions)
- 3 tablespoons Thai fish sauce seasoning
- 1 cup Thai basil
- 2 teaspoons coarsely ground black pepper
- 1/4 cup grated Parmesan cheese (optional)

Roast bell peppers on gas burner, or grill, or under broiler until blistered on all sides, turning frequently. Transfer to a paper or plastic bag, close and let them sweat at least 15 minutes. This will help loosen up the skins. Peel, seed and remove membrane of the peppers and slice them into small strips.

Bring water to a boil in a medium stockpot with vegetable oil and salt. Add pasta, stirring pasta occasionally to prevent it from sticking together and cook until *al dente*, about 7 minutes, drain and set aside.

Heat olive oil in a large saucepan over medium heat. Add sliced garlic, Kee Noo chili flakes and stir for a minute. Add wine and sauté until reduced in half. Add tomatoes, lemongrass stock, fish sauce and bring to a boil for 2 to 3 minutes. Add pasta and stir constantly for 2 minutes. Remove and transfer to a pasta bowl. Toss roasted pepper and Thai basil on top and sprinkle with black pepper. Add cheese if desired.

Bon appetito! ❖

● Waterfall in Samui Island.

● Koh Samui (koh means island in Thai)

QUICK CUISINE

Koh Samui Coconut Heaven

Koh Samui is located 18 miles off the coast of Surat Thani. Koh Samui, together with 40 others makes up a chain of islands known as the Ang-Thong Archipelago. Koh Samui is Thailand's third largest island. Samui is known for its long white sand beaches, aquamarine waters and sleepy lagoons fringed with the coconut palm trees that make this island one of Southeast Asia's premier resorts. There are 11 magnificent beaches to choose from. Some are isolated and tranquil while others are popular and lively.

Koh Samui is a water lover's paradise. Here you can participate in every water sport imaginable. Sailing, jet skiing, scuba diving, snorkeling, water skiing and sea kayaking. And if you're up for more adventure, you can elephant trek to one of the many waterfalls on the island.

Located on the island's north shore "sits" one of Samui's main landmarks, the Big Buddha of Wat Phra Yai. The Big Buddha is a whopping 40 feet tall. The locals built it in 1972 to give visitors a place to pay respect to the Lord Buddha. The small town of Nathon serves as Samui's capital and a sight worth seeing are the colorful fishing boats in the harbor.

The island is thickly covered with coconut and durian plantations. The traditional occupation of Samui's 40,000 residents is working in Samui's thriving coconut industry. Approximately 2 million coconuts are shipped to Bangkok monthly. Some growers have specially trained monkeys who harvest the coconuts. The monkeys select only the coconuts that are ready to be picked. They spin them until they fall to the ground. The coconuts grown on Koh Samui are some of the best in the kingdom.

I'll never forget the day we videotaped coconut harvesting on one of the plantations. I watched in amazement as a woman was shelling coconuts. She was surrounded by huge piles of coconuts. She picked them up one at a time and slammed the heavy coconut against a metal stake that was sticking out of the ground. Then using the stake she pried loose the thick husk. She tossed the husk in one direction and the shelled coconut in another. Using this rhythmic technique she shells an astounding 1,000 coconuts a day, by hand.

As I stood and watched I couldn't help but think of one of my favorite Thai treats, coconut ice cream. At that very moment a vendor on a motorbike appeared on the path with a cart of fresh homemade coconut ice cream. I was in coconut heaven!

Joanne Durfee

Asparagus Shrimp Fried Rice

I made this dish one day when I had shrimp and asparagus left over in the refrigerator. I heated it up and instead of pouring it over the cooked Jasmine rice as usual, I added the rice to the pan. The result was quite good and it's so easy to make. Now, lets find what other things are left over in the fridge and make some fun dishes with them.

❖ *Recipe serves 1*

- 1 teaspoon virgin olive oil
- $\frac{1}{2}$ teaspoon salt-free Thai seasoning
- 8 shrimp, shelled and deveined (size 21-26 per lb.)
- 1 tablespoon virgin olive oil
- 1 teaspoon finely chopped garlic
- $\frac{1}{3}$ cup thinly sliced red onion
- 1 cup asparagus, peeled and cut into $1\frac{1}{2}$ inch lengths
- $1\frac{1}{2}$ cups cooked Jasmine rice
- 1 tablespoon oyster sauce
- 2 teaspoons Thai fish sauce seasoning
- 4 whole yellow or red cherry tomatoes cut in half
- 1 whole red jalapeno or Serrano chili thinly sliced into long strips
- 3 tablespoons vegetable stock or water
- $\frac{1}{2}$ teaspoon cracked black pepper

Combine olive oil, shrimp and Thai seasoning in a bowl, mix thoroughly, and set aside. Place olive oil and garlic into a skillet over high heat. Add shrimp and sauté for 2 minutes or until shrimp turns pinkish in color. Add red onion, asparagus and rice. Stir constantly for 3 minutes. Add oyster sauce, fish sauce, tomatoes, jalapeno chili and vegetable stock. Stir constantly for 2 minutes until ingredients are thoroughly mixed. Remove to a serving plate and sprinkle with cracked black pepper. ❖

● Ang Thong National Marine Park, Surat Thani, Thailand.

Aisha Noodles

This is my daughter Aisha's favorite rice noodle dish. When we go out for lunch, her sister, Chyna will order her Pink Noodles, Aisha will order this dish and I will order whatever my heart desires. Aisha will order Chicken Noodles with no chicken, but add straw mushrooms and baby corn with no MSG. Go figure! The servers always get a headache.

❖ *Recipe serves 1*

- 1 tablespoon olive oil
- 4 oz. fresh rice noodles or dried Rad Na noodles (see glossary page 204)
- 1/2 teaspoon Thai fish sauce seasoning
- 1 teaspoon sweet black bean sauce

Sauce

- 1 tablespoon olve oil
- 1 teaspoon chopped fresh garlic
- 2 teaspoons fermented dark bean condiment
- 1/2 cup baby corn
- 1/4 cup straw mushrooms
- 1 1/2 cups Asian broccoli cut into bite-size pieces
- 1 cup chicken stock or vegetable (see page195 for instructions)
- 1 tablespoon oyster sauce
- 1 tablespoon Thai fish sauce seasoning
- 2 teaspoons sugar
- 1 tablespoon rice vinegar
- 1/4 teaspoon ground white pepper
- 3 teaspoons tapioca flour or cornstarch
- 3 tablespoons cold water
- 1 1/2 tablespoons finely diced chili vinegar (see page 192 for instructions)
- 1/4 teaspoon dried Kee Noo chili flakes

Place olive oil in a skillet over high heat. Add noodles and stir for a minute and add fish sauce, sweet black bean sauce and stir for 2 minutes. Remove and transfer to a serving plate.

Combine olive oil, garlic and bean condiment in a skillet over medium heat and stir for a minute. Add baby corn, straw mushrooms and stir for a minute. Add broccoli and stir for a minute. Add chicken stock, oyster sauce, fish sauce, sugar, vinegar, white pepper, and bring sauce to a boil. Dissolve tapioca in the water and slowly add to boiling sauce mixture stirring constantly to prevent sauce from becoming lumpy and cook for 2 to 3 minutes or until sauce thickens. Remove to a serving plate. Add diced chili vinegar and chili flakes as desired. Aisha likes them spicier. ❖

Asian Sausage Fried Rice

When you shop at Asian markets you will find this sausage in the refrigerated section. They look like small sausage links but feel hard when you squeeze them. I had a chance to visit the factory to see how they make them. First, they mix ground pork with spices and put it in a casing, then transfer the sausages to a huge smokehouse to smoke for 2 days, then cool. I used to help my father grill this sausage at his sidewalk café near the Grand Central Train Station in Bangkok. It smelled soooo good!

❖ *Recipe serves 1*

- 1 tablespoon olive oil
- 1 link of Chinese sausage 2 inches in length, thinly sliced at a 45° angle
- 1 teaspoon finely chopped garlic
- 4 whole dried shiitake mushrooms soaked in water, sliced into $^1/_4$ inch strips
- $1^1/_2$ cups cooked Jasmine rice (see page 191)
- $^1/_4$ cup thinly sliced red bell peppers
- $^1/_4$ cup thinly diced tender celery
- 2 teaspoons Thai light soy sauce
- $1^1/_2$ teaspoons sweet black bean sauce or sweet soy sauce
- 1 teaspoon Thai fish sauce seasoning
- $^1/_8$ teaspoon ground white pepper
- 2 tablespoons reserved mushroom water
- 2 tablespoons Italian parsley leaves (substitute with cilantro leaves)
- 2 tablespoons crispy ginger (see page 193)
- $^1/_4$ cup shredded scallions 3 inches in length and soaked in ice-cold water to allow them to curl

Place olive oil into a skillet over high heat. Add Chinese sausage and stir for 2-3 minutes until the sliced sausage is charred outside. Add garlic and mushrooms and stir for 1 minute. Add rice, bell pepper and celery and stir for 2 minutes. Add soy sauce, sweet black bean sauce, fish sauce, white pepper and stir constantly for 3 minutes. Remove to a serving plate and sprinkle parsley leaves and crispy ginger on top of the sausage-fried rice and garnish with curled scallions. ❖

● **Chiang Mai sausage street vendor.**

Thai Omelet Over Rice

When I want something quick and don't really have time to prepare a complicated meal, this is it. I remember my college days, when I didn't have enough money to eat out or buy fish or meat. I cooked this dish for many weeks. Thai people love this as an easy one-plate meal or they will have it as part of a multiple course menu. You can add cheese or other veggies and remove items you don't like, as long as you serve it with Seracha chili pepper sauce.

❖ *Serves 1*

- 1 1/2 cups cooked Jasmine rice (see page 191)
- 2 tablespoons olive oil
- 3 large eggs beaten
- 2 tablespoons cold water
- 1/3 cup thinly sliced brown onions
- 2 tablespoons finely diced red bell pepper
- 1/4 cup finely sliced scallions
- 2 tablespoons chopped Italian parsley or cilantro leaves
- 1 tablespoon Thai fish sauce seasoning
- 1 teaspoon Tommy's Thai seasoning
- 1/4 cup Thai Seracha chili pepper sauce
- 2 tablespoons Grated Asiago or Parmesan cheese

Combine egg, water, scallions, parsley, cheese, Thai seasoning and fish sauce. Beat thoroughly to mix, then set aside. Heat olive oil in a skillet over medium heat. Add brown onion and stir for a minute. Pour egg mixture into the skillet over brown onion. Reduce heat to low and cook undisturbed for 3 minutes. Flip egg over and cook for 2-3 minutes or until you see runny egg disappear. Remove and transfer cooked Thai omelet to plate of steamy Jasmine rice and serve with Seracha pepper sauce. ❖

● **Gor-lae, Samui Island fishing boat.**

Late Night Noodle Snack

When I was writing this book in Angola, near Buffalo City, NY late at night, I mean real late, about 3:00 a.m. ..., I was a little bit hungry, but I didn't want to take too long to cook. That evening, I prepared dinner of ginger fried rice and pepper-coated swordfish with basil curry. I still had some leftover ingredients and this was my creation. So double it for 2 and for 4 calculate by yourself.

❖ *Serves 1*

- 3 oz. Mee Krob noodles
- 4 cups boiling water
- 2 slices hard salami or lean bacon strips, diced into small pieces
- 1 tablespoon Thai fish sauce seasoning
- 1 tablespoon Thai sweet black bean sauce
- 2 tablespoons crispy garlic with olive oil (see page 192 for instructions)
- 1 tablespoon lime juice
- 2 tablespoons crispy shallots (see page 192 for instructions)
- 3 tablespoons finely sliced scallions
- 5 whole basil leaves torn into small pieces
- 1/2 teaspoon Thai chili flakes (optional remember, it's late at night!)

Pour boiling water over Mee Krob noodles in a bowl (make sure noodles are immersed in hot water) soak for 5 minutes, drain and transfer to another bowl and set aside.

While noodles are soaking in hot water, place salami or bacon in a small skillet and cook until it turns crispy. Remove and place on a paper towel to remove excess grease.

Place crispy salami or bacon on top of the noodles, add remaining ingredients and eat. ❖

● Santiburi Resort, Samui Island.

Roasted Chili Fried Rice

When I'm hungry and in hurry and want a quick fix but with good flavor, I'll whip up this dish. If you have a well stocked pantry of your favorite Thai ingredients, this recipe is very quick and easy to make. You will love it, trust me! Just try, your mouth will be so happy.

❖ *Recipe serves 1*

- 1 tablespoon virgin olive oil
- 1 teaspoon finely chopped garlic
- 3 oz. minced chicken breast (optional)
- 2 teaspoons Thai roasted chili paste
- 1 whole Serrano or jalapeno chili thinly sliced in strips (optional)
- 1 1/2 cups cooked Jasmine rice (I prefer left over rice)
- 1/4 cup diced red bell pepper
- 3 tablespoons small diced zucchini
- 1/2 cup sliced brown onion
- 2 teaspoons Thai fish sauce seasoning
- 1/4 cup Thai basil or regular basil
- 3 tablespoons lemongrass stock, vegetable stock or water (see page 196)
- 1 tablespoon very finely sliced Kaffir lime leaves (about 2 Kaffir lime leaves)
- 2 tablespoons crispy shallots (see page 192)
- 1 sprig Thai basil for garnish

Place garlic and olive oil into a skillet over high heat and sauté for 1 minute. Add chicken and stir for 2-3 minutes, until chicken is half cooked. Add chili paste, Serrano chili, and stir for a minute. Add cooked Jasmine rice, bell pepper, zucchini and brown onion, stir for 2-3 minutes. Add fish sauce, basil leaves and lemongrass stock; stir constantly for 2 minutes. Remove to a serving plate. Sprinkle with Kaffir lime leaves and crispy shallots. Garnish with basil sprig and serve. ❖

● Santiburi Resort private beach.

Northern Express Crab Fried Rice

I'll never forget the first time I ate Crab Fried Rice. I was traveling on the northern train to the city of Lum-Parng near Chiang Mai. When I close my eyes I can still remember the taste. When I went to Thailand to tape my TV cooking show, I convinced my director, Tom, and my producer, Joanne, to board the train to Lum-Parng with me. Guess what I ordered for dinner?

❖ *Recipe serves 1*

- 1 tablespoon olive oil
- 3 tablespoons thinly sliced shallots
- 1/2 cup cooked crab meat
- 1 egg beaten
- 1 1/2 cups cooked Jasmine rice
- 1/4 cup small diced brown onions
- 1/4 cup finely diced seeded tomatoes
- 1 teaspoon Thai light soy sauce
- 2 teaspoons fish sauce seasoning
- 1/4 teaspoon sugar
- 1/4 teaspoon ground white pepper
- 2 tablespoons vegetable stock or water
- 1 tablespoon lime or lemon juice
- 2 tablespoons finely cut chives
- 3 tablespoons sliced cilantro leaves
- 1 tablespoon roasted garlic (no oil)
- 4 sprigs cilantro for garnish

Place shallots and oil into a skillet over high heat and stir for 2 minutes. Add crab and beaten egg; leave undisturbed for 1 to 2 minutes. Gently scramble the egg until it is still in small lumps. Add rice, onions, and tomatoes and stir for 2 minutes. Add soy sauce, fish sauce, sugar, white pepper, vegetable stock, and lime juice, stirring constantly until ingredients are mixed thoroughly, 2 to 3 minutes. Remove to a serving plate, sprinkle chives and cilantro leaves over rice. Toss crispy garlic on top and garnish with cilantro.❖

● **Bangkok, Grand Central Train Station.**

Silver Noodle Shrimp

I prefer to use silver noodles instead of rice noodles or cooked rice as part of this dish. As a matter of fact, if you like Pad Thai noodles, substitute rice stick noodles for silver noodles, it will taste lighter, and you'll love it.

❖ *Recipe serves 1*

- 1 1/2 tablespoons olive oil
- 5 large shrimp, shelled and deveined (size 21-25 shrimp per lb.)
- 1 egg beaten
- 1/3 cup sliced brown onions
- 1/4 cup diced celery
- 1/4 cup shredded carrots
- 3 tablespoons sliced red bell pepper
- 1/4 cup sliced button mushrooms
- 2 oz. silver noodles
- 3 tablespoons vegetarian or chicken stock (see page 195)
- 1/2 teaspoon salt free Thai seasoning
- 1/2 teaspoon Thai sweet black bean sauce
- 2 teaspoons Thai fish sauce seasoning
- 1 tablespoon lime or lemon juice
- 2 tablespoons sliced parsley leaves
- 1 tablespoon ground roasted peanuts
- 1 tablespoon crispy garlic (see page 192)
- 1 teaspoon chili oil (see page 190)
- 1 tablespoon finely cut chives
- 1 sprig parsley for garnish

Blanch silver noodles in 2 cups of boiling water for 2 to 3 minutes. Strain and rinse with cold water and set aside.

Place olive oil into a skillet over high heat. Add shrimp and sauté for 1 minute until shrimp turns pinkish in color. Add beaten egg and leave undisturbed for 1-2 minutes. Scramble gently until egg has small lumps. Add onions, celery, carrots, red bell peppers and mushrooms. Stir for 1-2 minutes. Add silver noodles, stock, Thai seasoning, fish sauce, black bean sauce, and lime juice, stirring constantly for 2-3 minutes. Add parsley and stir until mixed thoroughly.

Remove to a serving plate. Sprinkle with ground peanuts and roasted garlic. Splash chili oil over noodles and toss diced chives around the plate and garnish with parsley. ❖

Smoked Sausage Fried Rice with Holy Basil

I love grilled sausages. Any kind of sausages, from meats, poultry to seafood, I love them all. When I lived in New York City, I went to the San Gennero Festival in Little Italy, near Canal Street, with my friend Gerard. We ate tons of Italian food that night but the dish I loved the most was grilled smoked sausage. That is why I made this recipe for you.

❖ *Recipe serves 1*

- 1 tablespoon olive oil
- 2 teaspoons finely chopped garlic
- 2 whole crushed fresh Kee Noo chili or Serrano chili
- 1/3 cup thinly sliced smoked sausage
- 1 1/2 cups cooked brown rice
- 1/4 cup sliced brown onions
- 1/3 cup yellow or red cherry tomatoes cut in half
- 1/4 cup shredded carrots
- 1/4 cup thinly sliced red bell pepper
- 2 tablespoons thinly sliced lemongrass
- 1/2 tablespoon Thai sweet black bean sauce
- 1 tablespoon Thai fish sauce seasoning
- 2 tablespoons lemongrass or vegetable stock
- 1/4 cup holy basil leaves
- 1/8 teaspoon ground white pepper

Place garlic and olive oil into a skillet over high heat and sauté for 1 minute. Add Kee Noo chili and sausages and stir for 1 minute. Add brown rice, brown onion, carrot, bell pepper and lemongrass and stir for 2 to 3 minutes. Add sweet black bean sauce, fish sauce and lemongrass stock and stir for a minute. Add holy basil and white pepper and stir for 2 minutes. Remove to a plate and garnish with a sprig of basil. ❖

● A quick nap while taping my TV show.

Roasted Garlic Pasta with Meng-Luck Basil

When I was in Thailand for a month taping my show for Public TV, I was homesick. Yes, I mean "America"! I ate so much Thai food and was not just missing my family, but was dying to have a plate of pasta. While sitting in a restaurant with my TV production crew in the wonderful Montien Riverside Hotel in Bangkok, I looked at the menu, but nothing really turned me on. I asked to speak to the restaurant chef. "Do you have Italian pasta?" I asked. He said that he could get some from the restaurant next door. So I gave him the recipe run down. One question he asked, "Is the olive oil the same as we use for hair tonic?" I replied, "Yes, that's the one!" He went back shaking his head. Twenty minutes later, I got my bowl of pasta made just the way I like it. It made my homesickness more digestible. The chef came back to the table and I asked him, "Will you remember this for the next time?" The whole table just cracked up. And now you can try it too!

❖ *Recipe serves 1*

- 6 large cloves of garlic, skin intact
- 3 oz. linguine
- 5 cups water
- 1/4 teaspoon sea salt
- 1 1/2 tablespoons garlic olive oil (see page 192)
- 1/3 tablespoon liquid from cooking pasta
- 1/2 teaspoon Kee-Noo chili flakes (substitute with other hot chili flakes)
- 2 teaspoons Thai fish sauce seasoning
- 1/2 cup Meng Luck basil (sorry, no substitute!)

Place the 6 cloves of garlic on a sheet of aluminum foil and fold to cover garlic. Make 3-4 folds then squeeze to make it airtight. Place wrapped garlic on a grill or burner with or without wire rack and grill for 5 to 6 minutes on each side over low heat. Unwrap, discard skin and set aside.

Place water and salt into a stockpot over high heat and bring to a boil. Add pasta and cook for 8 minutes, drain and set aside, reserving 1/3 cup pasta cooking water for the sauce.

Place garlic olive oil and grilled garlic into a skillet over medium heat. Mash the garlic and sauté for 2 minutes. Add pasta, salt, fish sauce, and liquid from cooked pasta and stir for 2-3 minutes. Add chili flakes and Meng Luck basil. Toss until thoroughly mixed and transfer to a pasta bowl. ❖

Stone Forest Tofu

From time to time I feel a little overweight. (I just feel it but I am, by no means, really heavy) I cook this dish 3 to 4 times a week. The soybean in the tofu and the rice combine to make an energizing complete protein. Fresh ginger, Thai basil and chili really give it a kick. This spicy tofu over Thai Jasmine brown rice is what I use for both spa and comfort food. I can just look at this recipe and feel slimmer already.

❖ *Recipe serves 1*

$1\frac{1}{2}$ tablespoons virgin olive oil	$\frac{1}{2}$ tablespoon Thai light soy sauce
1 tablespoon chopped garlic	$\frac{1}{4}$ cup sliced red bell pepper
2 tablespoons chopped red onions	$\frac{1}{4}$ cup diced tomatoes
1 tablespoon chopped, peeled fresh ginger	$\frac{1}{2}$ cup lemongrass stock (see page 196)
1 tablespoon finely chopped Serrano chili	$\frac{1}{2}$ cup Thai basil leaves
1 cup diced firm white or brown tofu	$1\frac{1}{2}$ cups Jasmine white or brown rice (see page 191 for instructions)
1 tablespoon Thai fish sauce seasoning	

Place olive oil and garlic into a skillet over high heat and stir for a minute. Add onions, ginger, Serrano chili and stir for 2 minutes. Add tofu, fish sauce, soy sauce, bell pepper, tomatoes, lemongrass stock and stir for 3-4 minutes. Add basil and stir until mixed thoroughly. Serve spicy tofu over steamy hot Jasmine white or brown rice.

Have a great protein day. ❖

Wat Phra That Doi Suthep, Chiang Mai.

SOMETHING NICE

Chiang Mai is located in the north and is the second largest city in Thailand. King Meng Rai with the help of his two buddies, King Phor Khoon Ram Khum Haeng the Great of the Sukhothai Kingdom and King Praya Ngam Muang of Prayao, built Chiang Mai. The three friends chose the fertile plains between Suthep Mountain and the Ping River as the site of the new city. They built it to replace the old city that was called "Wiang Kumkham", which was located in Sarapee district, Chiang Mai province. The construction was completed in 1296 and they named the new city "Nopburi Sri Nakhon Ping Chiang Mai" or Chiang Mai for short. The word Chiang means city and the word Mai means new, very appropriate, to name it "new city". In 1996, Chiang Mai cerebrated its 700th anniversary and I was there to tape my TV show for public television.

The climate in Chiang Mai is milder than Bangkok, but the winter can be very cold, especially on the high mountains where most ethnic minorities live. Due to this cooler climate, Chiang Mai is also known as "The Rose of The North". Wild flowers bloom everywhere in the forest. At the end of January and beginning of February, every year, the city celebrates with its own Flower Festival and "Rose Parade". Many Thais and visitors from around the globe come here to celebrate.

Chiang Mai is also known as the arts and crafts capital of Thailand, for such industries as silk making, silver, celadon pottery, jade and wood carving, especially the carving of elephants. People in Chiang Mai are very gentle, speak their own native northern dialect and talk slower than people in other regions in Thailand. Sometimes I feel that they talk too slowly and too politely! There is always something nice to do here, like visiting Doi Suthep Temple, visiting hill tribes, and elephant trekking, which is one of my favorite thing to do.

Tommy

• Hilltribes village, Golden Triangle.

Tommy's Potato Latkes

We always celebrate CHANUKKAH (you can spell it HANUKKAH) every year in our home. And every year as part of the celebration we serve Potato Latkes at our table. One year I was complaining about how bad and mushy the latkes were that we brought from the local deli. I kept complaining throughout the meal until my lovely wife Sandi couldn t stand it. She simply told me, why don t you make them next year?

To her surprise, I made these a year later. Enjoy! Happy CHANUKKAH.

❖ *Recipe serves 6 to 8*

- 8 cups potatoes thinly shredded
- 2 cups onions finely chopped
- 2 large eggs
- 3 tablespoons all purpose flour
- 3 tablespoons rice flour
- 2 tablespoons Thai fish sauce seasoning (or 2 teaspoons sea salt)
- 1 tablespoon salt-free Thai seasoning (see glossary page 205)
- 2 tablespoons granulated garlic
- 1 cup olive oil for frying
- $1\frac{1}{2}$ cups sour cream
- $1\frac{1}{2}$ cups apple sauce
- $\frac{1}{3}$ cup thinly diced chives or scallions

Place potato mixture ingredients into a bowl and mix thoroughly and set aside.

Place 2 tablespoons of olive oil into a large nonstick skillet over medium low heat. Add a small amount of the potato mixture into the hot skillet and spread thinly (like a pancake) to form a 3 to 4 inch circle, and cook until edges are brown. Flip and cook until both sides turn crispy. Drain on rack over paper towels and keep warm. Repeat until the potato mixture is finished.

Place small amount of applesauce on a piece of potato latke; add sour cream and sprinkle chives on top. Happy Holidays. ❖

● **Chanukkah candle holder.**

Stuffed Chicken Breast
with Dried Fruits, Walnuts & Pineapple Mango Chutney

If you never stuffed a chicken breast, you may find yourself uncertain and not wanting to try to do this dish. Please don t feel bad; once I felt like you. Through trial and error I was able to do it. The secret is not to use too much stuffing, and use bamboo skewers to hold it all together.

❖ *Recipe serves 4 to 6*

Marinade

- 6 pieces boneless half chicken breast 7 to 8 oz. each skin in tact
- 2 tablespoons virgin olive oil
- 2 tablespoons finely chopped garlic
- $1\frac{1}{2}$ teaspoons sea salt
- $1\frac{1}{2}$ teaspoons cracked black pepper
- 2 tablespoons finely minced fresh or dried rosemary

Stuffing

- 1 cup mixed dried fruits, mango, peach, pear, apple, pineapple or cherry
- $\frac{1}{2}$ cup roasted, chopped, unsalted walnuts
- $\frac{1}{2}$ cup finely diced red bell pepper
- 1 cup finely diced portabello mushrooms or shiitake mushrooms
- $\frac{1}{4}$ cup finely diced shallots
- 1 teaspoon sea salt
- 8-6 inches bamboo skewers soaked in water for an hour
- 2 tablespoons olive oil for searing

Chutney

- 2 cups chopped, fresh ripe mango
- 1 whole pineapple, flesh chopped into small pieces
- 10 cloves garlic, skin removed and gently cracked
- 1 stick cinnamon, 4 to 5 inches
- 6 whole cloves
- 2 teaspoons sea salt
- 2 tablespoons brown sugar
- 2 cups fresh water
- 4 fresh mint sprigs for garnish

Use a small knife to make an incision in the middle of the chicken breast, deep enough to hold $\frac{1}{4}$ cup of stuffing and set aside.

Combine chicken and marinade ingredients in a bowl, coat chicken thoroughly and set aside in the refrigerator for 1 hour.

Meanwhile, place chutney ingredients in a small stockpot and bring to a boil. Reduce heat to low and simmer for 35 to 40 minutes or until chutney becomes thick. Remove and set aside.

Combine stuffing ingredients in a mixing bowl and divide into 6 even portions. Stuff the mixture into the chicken breast pocket and close with bamboo skewers.

Place olive oil into a large skillet over medium high heat. Add stuffed chicken breasts skin side down and sear for 2 to 3 minutes. Remove and transfer seared chicken breast to a pre-heated oven at 375°F. for 40 to 45 minutes. Remove baked stuffed chicken breast to a cutting board. With a sharp knife, slice stuffed chicken breasts into bite-size pieces, arrange in a circle on the platter and serve with mango and pineapple chutney. Garnish with fresh mint sprigs.❖

Wild Mushroom Polenta

Don t even try to look for this recipe in other Thai restaurants in your area. This is not in the typical Thai repertoire. I always enjoy creating something new. I know you ve had Polenta before somewhere else, but I guarantee, you ve never had mine.

❖ *Recipe serves 4*

- 2 1/2 cups water
- 1 1/2 cups milk
- 1 can (14 oz.) coconut milk
- 2 teaspoons granulated garlic
- 2 teaspoons sea salt
- 1/2 teaspoon ground white pepper
- 2 cups coarse cornmeal (same size as granulated sugar)
- 1 cup cooked corn kernels
- 1/4 cup ** Thai black rice (substitute with Canadian wild rice)
- 1/4 cup very small diced red bell peppers
- 3/4 cup grated Parmesan cheese
- 2 tablespoons virgin olive oil
- 4-8 inch veal sausage links (optional)
- 1 tablespoon finely chopped garlic
- 2 cups mixed mushrooms, shiitake, oyster, chanterelle, portobello or button
- 3/4 cup sliced brown onions
- 1/2 cup diced, seeded tomatoes
- 1/4 cup very finely diced red bell peppers
- 1 tablespoon Thai light soy sauce
- 1 tablespoon rice vinegar
- 1/4 teaspoon sea salt
- 1 cup vegetable stock or fresh water
- 2 tablespoons finely chopped cilantro or Italian parsley

Place water, milk, coconut milk, garlic, salt and white pepper into a large deep stockpot or steamer. (Use non-stick, if you have one) and bring to a boil. Add cornmeal little at a time and keep stirring until cornmeal is lump free. Reduce heat to medium and stir constantly until it starts to pull away from the side of the pot, about 8 to 10 minutes. Add corn kernels, black rice, red pepper and cheese. Stir constantly until ingredients are thoroughly mixed and polenta is hard to stir, about 2 minutes. Transfer polenta to a baking dish 12 x 14 inches, smooth polenta and let it cool completely. Cut into 8 even square pieces.

Place sausage and half a tablespoon of olive oil into a skillet over medium heat and keep turning until sausage turns brown outside, about 6 to 8 minutes. Remove and cut each sausage link into 4 slices at a 45-degree angle and set aside. With the same skillet add 1 tablespoon of olive oil, garlic and mushrooms over high heat and sauté for 3 to 4 minutes. Add onions, tomatoes, bell peppers and sauté for 2 to 3 minutes. Add vegetable stock, salt, soy sauce and rice vinegar, stir and bring sauce to a boil. Reduce heat to medium low and let it simmer for 7 to 8 minutes or until sauce reduces by half.

While sauce simmers on the burner, place the remaining oil into a skillet over medium high heat. Place 2 to 4 pieces of polenta on the skillet. (Save other 4 pieces for next time) sear polenta 3 to 4 minutes each side. Transfer seared polenta to 4 serving plates and pour mushroom sauce over Thai polenta. Extra polenta can keep in the refrigerator up to a week. Freeze them for longer use.

****P**lace Thai black rice and 2 cups of water into a small stockpot over high heat and bring to a boil, reduce heat to medium high and cook for 15 minutes. Remove, drain and rinse with cold water and set aside.

*** **W**hen cooking polenta, please do not allow children to stir while cornmeal is bubbling, it can accidentally jump at you, so please be very careful. ❖

Khan-Toke dinner

When you visit Chiang-Mai for the first time, you must go to a Khan-Toke dinner. In the old days the citizens of Chiang-Mai welcomed their honored guests by serving Khan-Toke dinner and it became the city custom and tradition. Your meal will consist of Hung Lay curry, (similar to Mandalay curry), Northern Fried Chicken, Chiang-Mai style sausage and of course Chiang-Mai's famous dipping sauces. The food will come to you in an array of different size celadon bowls, on a high round tray. The tray will be placed on the middle of the floor mat with triangle pillows on the side. The guests will sit on the floor around the tray next to the pillows which will act as a cushion for you to lean on when you've had too much to eat or just to relax your back. With the Khan-Toke are local folk dances, to help you digest your meal. This definitely is one of my favorite meals in Thailand.

Crispy Whole Bass with Thai Chili Fish Sauce

Thais love to eat foods that are crispy, the crispier the better. To make something crispier, first you fry, and then let it cool and fry again. This time it will get crispier. Am I telling you to do the same thing with this fish? Yes and No. I like my fish crispy but also only outside. It must be moist and juicy inside. You can make another dish from this crispy fish by removing the bone and tearing the fish to small pieces. Add some crisp salad greens, crunchy sliced onions, all the topping ingredients plus Thai chili fish sauce. Now you have just created Crispy Fish Salad, how about that....

❖ *Recipe serves 4*

- 2 whole freshwater striped bass (2-2 1/2 lb.) gutted, scaled, rinsed and patted dry
- 6 cups vegetable oil for deep frying

Sauce

- 1/4 cup finely chopped Kee Noo chilies
- 1 teaspoon finely chopped garlic
- 2 teaspoons thinly sliced fresh Kaffir lime leaves
- 1/4 cup Thai fish sauce seasoning
- 1/3 cup lime or lemon juice
- 1/2 teaspoon palm sugar

Topping

- 1 cup crispy garlic (see page 192 for instructions)
- 1 cup crispy shallots (see page 192 for instructions)
- 1 cup crispy ginger (see page 193 for instructions)
- 1 cup crispy leeks (see page 193 for instructions)

With a sharp knife, gently make 3 to 4 incision marks on each side of the fish. Place oil into a large deep skillet over medium low heat. Slowly slide fish into hot oil and fry 7 to 8 minutes on each side. Remove crispy fish to a paper towel-lined tray to remove excess oil. Transfer fish to a serving plate and garnish with crispy garlic, shallots, ginger, and leeks.

To make Thai chili fish sauce: simply combine ingredients in a sauce bowl, mix thoroughly and serve.❖

● **The Dai (Thai) people originally from the southern Yunnan province, People Republic of China were The settlers in Thailand and still reside in China today.**

Grilled Seafood with Garlic Chili Vinegar Sauce

I love grilled fresh seafood and I like to invite my friends and bring my family to the island of either Samui or Phuket in the southern part of Thailand. I go to the harbor early in the morning and wait for the fisherman to haul in the night s catch. You cannot really buy directly from the fisherman, even though they would love to sell to you. We select and purchase the best catch of the day , fr om the seafood vendor, sounds like a restaurant menu board but sometimes you can t get a particular kind of fish. Today, cotton fish is what I really wanted, it s so soft, like cotton and the taste is marvelous. However, I had to settle for red snapper. Then we boarded my friend s boat and out we went to find the best beach with no Farang (Farang means foreigner) or local people around. We even have some banana and stale bread to feed the fish. My friend Tao and I set up the grill, while everybody swims and snorkels. The garlic chili vinegar sauce is so perfect for grilled seafood. We also bring sweet chili and garlic sauce with us. If you would like the recipe, you have to call or come to my restaurant to get it.

❖ *Recipe serves 4*

- 3 lbs. giant Thai tiger prawns 6-8 per lb. deveined, rinsed with shell intact
- 1-$1\frac{1}{2}$ lbs. whole snapper, sea or striped bass or other white fish, scales removed and rinsed
- 1 lb. small fresh calamari (squid) gutted, cleaned and rinsed
- 2 lbs. green or black mussels or clams
- $\frac{1}{2}$ cup olive oil
- 2 tablespoons salt-free Thai seasoning

Sauce

- 1 cup rice or vegetable vinegar
- 3 tablespoons fresh lime or lemon juice
- 10 cloves peeled garlic
- 4 whole Serrano chilies
- 2 teaspoons sea salt
- 2 teaspoons sugar
- 5 sprigs cilantro or flat leaf parsley

Brush prawns, fish and calamari with olive oil, thoroughly sprinkle Thai seasoning on them and set aside.

Prepare charcoal grill: put seafood on the grill for 8 to 9 minutes each side. For calamari grill until the transparency turns white, about 3 minutes each side. For mussels or clams, grill until they are completely opened.

Place sauce ingredients into a blender and blend until smooth. You can serve grilled seafood hot or at room temperature.

Garlic chili vinegar sauce can be kept in the refrigerator for up to 2 weeks.❖

● Fisherman harbon Phuket.

Mandalay Curry

Thailand s curry has had a major influence from India. Throughout centuries, Thais have adapted and constantly improved ways to prepare them. When you visit Thailand, you can find curry vendor stalls throughout the Kingdom. The key ingredient to making Thai curry is the curry paste. It is simply a mixture of chili, lemongrass, galanga, ginger, garlic, shallots, kaffir lime, cumin seeds and coriander seeds pounded with mortar and pestle into paste. This paste added to coconut milk, fish sauce and palm sugar, results in a simple Thai curry. You may add meats, fouls, seafood or vegetables of your choice. You will enjoy making these dishes as much as I do. Thais like to eat them with a hot steamy bowl of Thai Hom Mali Rice. jasmine rice .

❖ *Recipe serves 4 to 6*

- $1\frac{1}{2}$ lb. lamb, beef or chicken cut into 1 inch cubes
- 8 cups water
- $\frac{1}{4}$ cup vegetable oil
- 1 tablespoon red curry paste or panang curry paste
- 1 tablespoon roasted chili paste
- $1\frac{1}{2}$ tablespoons curry powder
- 2 cups coconut milk
- $\frac{1}{2}$ cup tamarind juice
- $1\frac{1}{2}$ tablespoons sweet black bean sauce (sweet soy sauce)
- 2 tablespoons Thai fish sauce seasoning
- $1\frac{1}{2}$ tablespoons palm or coconut sugar
- 4 whole bay leaves
- 1-4" inch cinnamon sticks
- 10 whole cardamom seeds
- 1 cup unsalted or raw macadamia nuts
- 8 whole white pearl onions or shallots, peeled
- 10 medium baby potatoes or 2 large potato cut to $1\frac{1}{4}$ inch cubes
- $\frac{1}{2}$ cup low fat yogurt
- 2-3 cups reserved lamb stock (add fresh water if needed)

Place lamb and water into a medium stockpot and bring to a boil. Reduce heat to low and simmer for 1 hour or until tender, remove and set aside.

Place oil, panang curry paste and roasted chili paste into a deep skillet over medium high heat, and stir for 1-$1\frac{1}{2}$ minutes. Add curry powder, $\frac{1}{4}$ cup coconut milk and stir for 1 to 2 minutes. Add remaining coconut milk, tamarind juice, sweet black bean sauce, fish sauce and palm sugar, bay leaves, cinnamon stick, cardamom seeds, stir and bring to boil. Reduce heat to medium low and simmer for 15 to 20 minutes. Add cooked lamb, macadamia nuts, pearl onions, potatoes, and yogurt and bring to a boil. Reduce heat to low and simmer for 30 to 45 minutes. Add lamb liquid if curry sauce is too dry. Remove to a large bowl and serve with cooked steamy hot Thai jasmine rice. ❖

Nam Prik Ong

This is the most famous dipping sauce in the Northern city of Chiang Mai. I have conducted many cooking classes in Chiang Mai over the years. Most of them included his sauce, along with Hung Lay curry, (similar to Mandalay curry) Northern Fried Chicken and sticky rice. Browsing through this book, you will find the recipes that I just mentioned. Invite your friends, neighbors and family over to make this northern-style cuisine together.

❖ *Recipe serves 4 to 6*

- 5 peeled shallots or medium red onions cut into 4 sections
- 6 cloves peeled garlic
- 2 cilantro roots or 6 sprigs cilantro stems and leaves
- $1\frac{1}{2}$ tablespoons vegetable oil
- $1\frac{1}{2}$ cups minced chicken or pork (optional)
- 1 tablespoon red or panang curry paste
- $1\frac{1}{2}$ cups diced tomatoes
- $\frac{1}{2}$ cup water
- 1 teaspoon honey or sugar
- $\frac{1}{2}$ teaspoon sea salt
- 2 tablespoons Thai fish sauce seasoning
- 2 tablespoons lime or lemon juice
- 1 small hot house or other cucumber
- 1 small green cabbage cut into small sections
- 2 large carrots peeled and cut into 4 inch sticks
- $\frac{1}{2}$ lb. okra
- $\frac{1}{2}$ lb. Thai long bean, French or regular string beans
- 3 cups pork rind (optional)

Wrap shallots and garlic in an aluminum sheet and fold tightly several times. Put them on a wire rack and grill on a low heat flame burner for 6 to 8 minutes. Remove, unwrap and put in a food processor or chop them coarsely with a knife and set aside.

Place vegetable oil into a skillet over medium heat, add minced chicken and curry paste. Stir for 2-3 minutes, add tomatoes, water and stir for 3-4 minutes. Add honey, salt, fish sauce, lime juice and bring mixture to a boil. Reduce heat to low and simmer for 17 to 20 minutes, stir occasionally, add more water if the sauce is too dry.

While dipping sauce is simmering, put 4 cups of water into a medium stockpot and bring to a boil. Add okra and long beans and boil for 3 minutes. Remove and rinse in cold water and set aside. Use fresh, blanched vegetables and pork rind to dip in the sauce.❖

● **Night Bazaar, Chiang Mai.**

Northern Fried Chicken

I named this Northern Fried Chicken because of its origin, the northern city of Chiang Mai. I believe in every corner of the town, you can find this deep fried bird and people who live there will tell you which one they think is the best. When I first came to live in New York City, all my friends argued and told me which pizza joint was the best in town. "Oh! Yes siree, I know the best pizza in New York." No! I'm not gonna tell you. "You have to find out yourself." That is the right way to do it. If you ask me where is the best Northern Fried Chicken is, I'll tell you. Come closer, a little bit closer; C-h-iang Mai, that's where!

❖ *Recipe serves 4*

- 2-1$^{1}/_{2}$ lbs whole chicken cleaned, rinsed and cut into small sections
- $^{1}/_{2}$ cup finely chopped garlic
- $^{1}/_{4}$ cup cilantro roots or stems with leaves finely chopped
- 3 teaspoons ground white pepper
- 3 teaspoons sea salt
- 2 cups all-purpose flour
- 6 cups vegetable oil for deep frying

Combine garlic, cilantro roots, 2 teaspoons of white pepper and 2 teaspoons of salt in a large mixing bowl. Rub chicken pieces with marinade mixture. Add $^{1}/_{2}$ cup of flour to rubbed chicken, coating thoroughly. Cover marinated chicken with plastic wrap and set aside in the refrigerator for 2 hours.

Place remaining pepper, salt and flour in a large plastic zipper bag. Add marinated chicken into bag, toss gently, remove and set aside.

Heat oil in a large deep skillet over medium high heat about 325°F.-350°F. Place half floured chicken into hot oil and fry for 8 to 10 minutes or until crisp and golden brown. Remove to a tray lined with paper towels to remove excess oil. Serve Northern Fried Chicken with Nam Prik Ong (recipe in this chapter) and steamed sticky rice. ❖

● **Come and walk up to Doi Suthep Temple with us, Chiang Mai.**

Seared Giant Tiger Prawns with Polenta & Mango Sauce

Some giant tiger prawns in Thailand are larger than lobster tails. Many visitors can't believe their own eyes when they see them. The way I like to cook them is simply grilled or seared. If you cook them too long they'll turn rubbery. This is a wonderful recipe to show off your skill and when you are making polenta, just be patient, it's worth the wait and it's to die for.

❖ *Recipe serves 4*

- 4 pieces Thai polenta (see page 168 for instructions)
- 4 whole giant tiger prawns 6-8 per lb. deveined, with the shell intact
- 3 tablespoons olive oil
- 1 tablespoon salt-free Thai seasoning
- 1 tablespoon finely chopped garlic
- 1 teaspoon Santa Fe chili powder
- $1\frac{1}{2}$ cups coconut milk
- $\frac{3}{4}$ cup finely diced, seeded tomatoes
- $\frac{1}{4}$ cup thinly sliced red bell pepper
- $\frac{1}{2}$ cup finely diced zucchini
- 1 cup sliced ripened mango
- 2 teaspoons Thai fish sauce seasoning
- $\frac{1}{4}$ cup sour cream
- 9 chives for garnish

Place tiger prawns into a mixing bowl, brush with 1 tablespoon of olive oil and sprinkle with Thai seasoning and set aside.

Place remaining olive oil into a deep skillet over medium heat. Add garlic and sauté for a minute, add Santa Fe chili powder, $\frac{1}{2}$ cup coconut milk and sauté for 2 minutes. Add tomatoes, red bell pepper, zucchini and sauté for 2 to 3 minutes and set aside.

Place mango and remaining coconut milk into a food blender. Add sauce into the blend until smooth. Transfer sauce to skillet, add sour cream and bring to a boil. Reduce heat to medium low and simmer for 6 to 7 minutes.

While sauce is simmering, place tiger prawns into a cast iron pan or griddle over high heat and sear each side for 3 minutes. Remove and set aside

Put polenta on 4 serving plates, arrange tiger prawns on top of polenta, pour mango curry sauce over prawns and polenta and garnish with chives. ❖

If you don't have a grill at home, you can use a griddle, and if you don't have a griddle, you can substitute with a cast iron pan. Please don't tell me you don't even have a cast iron pan. If you do not own one, I think it's time for you to buy it. It is American made and should last for a lifetime, if taken proper care of. The instructions for maintenance should come with it. In Thailand, some tiger prawn tails are larger than the lobster tails that you eat in restaurants in the U.S. For this recipe, if you buy extra large prawns you can use fewer of them.

Stir-Fried Guinea Hen with Macadamia Nut and Sweet Chili Hoisin Sauce

My friend James who used to live in Houston and now lives in San Francisco, called me about the new company where he works. He handles sales nationwide for a company that supplies Muscovy duck and Guinea hen. He sent me some samples to play with and I enjoyed them very much. Thank you James, this recipe is especially for you.

❖ *Recipe serves 4*

- 2 tablespoons olive oil
- 8 oz. minced guinea hen or free-range chicken
- 2 teaspoons finely chopped fresh garlic
- 1/2 cup small diced macadamia nuts
- 1/2 cup small diced water chestnuts
- 1/4 cup small diced portobello or shiitake mushrooms
- 1/4 cup small diced Anaheim chilies
- 1/4 cup small diced red bell pepper
- 1/4 cup small diced shallots or red onions
- 1 tablespoon sweet black bean sauce
- 1 tablespoon Thai fish sauce seasoning
- 1 tablespoon roasted sesame oil
- 1/2 teaspoon ground black pepper
- 1 teaspoon honey or sugar
- 1/2 cup chicken or vegetable stock or water
- 2 tablespoons thinly sliced chives or scallions
- 2 tablespoons minced parsley leaves
- 12 iceberg lettuce leaves or Boston lettuce or other lettuce leaves
- 2 oz. crispy Mee Krob noodles (see page 193 for instructions)

Chili Hoisin Sauce

- 1/2 cup Hoisin sauce
- 1 tablespoon sweet black bean sauce
- 2 teaspoons chili garlic oil (see page 190 for instructions)
- 2 teaspoons toasted white sesame seeds

Place olive oil, minced Guinea hen and garlic in a medium skillet over high heat and sauté for 3 to 4 minutes. Add remaining ingredients except scallions and parsley, stirring constantly for 3 minutes. Add scallions, parsley and stir until thoroughly mixed and transfer to a plate.

Combine sauce ingredients in a small dipping cup and mix it thoroughly and it's ready to be used.

Serving instruction: Spread a small amount of sweet chili hoisin sauce on a piece of lettuce, scoop a generous amount of stir-fried minced Guinea hen over sauce and put crispy Mee-Krob on top.

What are you waiting for? Eat.❖

Garlic Wasabi Mashed Potatoes

My wife Sandi loves garlic-mashed potatoes. At every restaurant we go to, if they serve these, she will order them. Sometimes you can only get them with an entr e and somehow she manages to convince the server to give it to her as a side dish. Sandi this is for you, babe!

❖ *Recipe serves 8*

2 lbs. potatoes	1/2 cup milk
12 cloves garlic, skin intact	3 teaspoons wasabi powder
4 tablespoons unsalted butter	1 teaspoon sea salt
3/4 cup coconut milk	1 1/2 tablespoons small diced chives
1/4 cup sliced ginger	

Preheat oven to 400°F. and bake potatoes in the oven for 50-55 minutes. Meanwhile, wrap garlic tightly in aluminum foil and grill on a wire rack or over medium low heat burner for 8 to 10 minutes. Remove, discard skin and set aside. When potatoes are done remove skins and place in a large bowl. Add roasted garlic, mash the cooked potatoes and set aside.

Heat butter, coconut milk, ginger, wasabi powder, milk and salt over medium heat and bring mixture to a boil. Reduce heat to low and simmer for 5 to 7 minutes.

Combine prepared mashed potatoes with coconut milk sauce mixture and stir for 4 to 5 minutes. Add chives and stir until thoroughly blended. Transfer Roasted Garlic Wasabi Mashed Potatoes to serving plates. Serve as a side dish, with chicken breast stuffed with mixed dried fruits and nuts on page 166 or with your other favorite dishes.❖

● **With my chef Keith Satha, @ Tommy Tang's restaurant.**

Sweet Yam Mousse with Coconut Ginger Sauce

Sit right here and let me tell you a story. I started to make this recipe many, many moons ago; I did this for a charity event that we participated in. The original recipe had dark chocolate in it. Later that same year, I prepared a Thanksgiving dinner for my family and friends. You know me; I have to do something different from other people. Instead of a turkey, I substituted with crispy baked Long Island duck with Sweet Yam Mousse. Very few people know the origin of this story, you know who you are and it took me many, many moons to get it in the cookbook.

❖ *Recipe serves 10 to 12*

3 lbs. yams	1/4 cup sliced ginger
4 tablespoons unsalted butter	1/2 cup milk
3/4 cup coconut milk	1/2 teaspoon sea salt

Preheat oven to 400°F. and bake yams in the oven for 45 minutes. Remove yam skins and place the rest in a large bowl, mash yams and set aside. Heat butter, coconut milk, ginger, milk and salt over medium heat. Bring mixture to a boil. Reduce heat to low and simmer for 5 minutes. Remove ginger. Pour coconut milk mixture over mashed yams.

Place mashed yams in a deep skillet over medium heat and stir until thoroughly blended. Serve yam mousse as a side dish for Tommy's Duck (recipe is in my first cookbook) or other entrées that you find appropriate. ❖

● Lady @ coconut plantation.

● Yes ! is me durain, the sticky fruit, but taste marvellous.

BASIC EASY RECIPIES

Exotic Fruit

On our first night in Bangkok, I was puzzled by a sign in the hotel lobby, and another on the inside of our door. It was a picture of a spiky looking object, like a blowfish, or a medieval mace, inside a circle with a diagonal line through it. "What does that mean?" I asked the bellhop. "No durian," he said, telling me that durian is a local fruit that smells so bad, you are forbidden to open one in your hotel room. I couldn't imagine! But I was curious.

Although our hotel does not allow durian, its breakfast buffet offered at least fifty different choices. There was a whole table with a rainbow of exotic fruits, sliced and garnished as if for a king. There were melons, citrus, strawberries, and other fruits familiar to westerners, but I was interested in the ones I'd never seen before. There was a bowl of fresh lychee in their natural juice, very lightly sweetened. The light, nutty, flowery taste had nothing to do with the soggy canned lychee in perfumery syrup of my previous experience. And then there was something shaped like small chayote squash, nearly triangular with a scalloped bottom. It was sweet/tart and crispy, close in flavor to an Asian pear. I looked for them as we drove past the street markets in Bangkok, and I felt like a child gawking at the dazzle of color and variety of fruit, vegetable, and flower offerings. Finally I found them. "They are called rose apples in English," Tommy said. "And where are the durians?" I asked. "Ohhhhhh," he said, in a cautioning tone, "the durians."

A few days later we are on our way to ride elephants into the jungle. Coconut trees line our way. Tommy saw a coconut vendor, the car stopped, and the next thing we know, Tommy is out and back with coconuts roasted in the husk by the roadside. He wants us to see and smell and taste Thailand in all its variety. He says roasting intensifies the coconut flavor, and it does. After lunch at the elephant camp, overlooking a beautiful river, we are brought sweet tamarind pods to crack open, and suck the sticky jam-like paste from the large seeds. The flavor is something like very ripe apricot leaning toward prune. I am addicted immediately. Tommy showed me where to buy them in Los Angeles and now I make a pilgrimage once a week.

The next day we descend from a magnificent temple, having been blessed by a monk, surrounded by golden spires and glittering mosaics. At the foot of the stairs, Tommy is waiting at the cart of a pineapple vendor with spears of dripping pineapple, cut into the shape of dragon's teeth. We have never tasted pineapple like this. It, too, must have been blessed.

In Chiang Mai that night, dining like royalty at Tommy's friend Nit's palatial house, which includes her restaurant, I asked her about durian. She said, "People either love it or hate it, and I love it. I think it tastes like butter cake." But she didn't have any. Instead she gave me a glass of starfruit juice. I will never forget each and every sip. What luxury. At the end of the meal the waiter brought a platter of another strange fruit, a mound of small saucer shaped disks the color of Halloween marshmallow peanuts. It's jackfruit. Nit had them cut it from her tree for us.

Back at our Bangkok hotel buffet, I noticed that next to the fresh lychee were other fresh lychee, but a little more oval shaped. I tried them. Divine. I got some more. I asked the maitre d' what the difference is. The oval ones are not lychee at all, but another fruit called rambutan, and I couldn't get enough of it. How sad I am to find that they are only available in the States in a can. Tommy always has an answer. Pour out the syrup. Rinse. Then put them in the freezer for half an hour to restore some texture.

Another night there was a huge food festival outdoors in a public park, sponsored by Singha beer, and there must have been 200 food stalls offering one temptation after another. We are with Tommy in Thailand, so of course we sit at the V.I.P. Singha table, where dish after dish is put under our noses. And finally, one of them is the dreaded durian.

Well, they're right. It smells foul. The sissies pull away. But I am undaunted. I taste. And I'm a little sorry. It tastes like hazelnut browned butter poured over my husband's gym socks. Then I remember that I am fond of many bad smelling French cheeses. The trick is to use the tongue more than the nose. I try again. It tastes a little more like butter cake this time. But I won't be trying to find a mail order source. If I make as many trips to Thailand as I hope to, I might learn to love durian.

Janet Spiegel

● Thai tropical fruits.

Chili Fish Sauce

- $^1/_4$ cup finely diced or chopped, fresh Kee Noo chili
- 1 teaspoon finely chopped garlic
- 2 teaspoons very finely sliced Kaffir lime leaves
- $^1/_4$ cup Thai fish sauce seasoning
- $^1/_4$ cup lime or lemon juice

Mix all ingredients thoroughly in a sauce cup and it ready to be used as an all-purpose dipping sauce or stored in a tightly closed container. This Chili Fish Sauce can be kept in the refrigerator up to a month. ❖

Diced Chili Vinegar

$^1/_2$ cup	Finely diced Serrano chilies	2 cloves	Fresh garlic
$^3/_4$ cup	Rice vinegar		

Combine ingredients in a jar and shake. Keep this chili vinegar in the refrigerator for later use, up to 3 months. ❖

Fresh Ground Red Chili Vinegar

- $^1/_3$ cup fresh ground red chilies (sambal oeleck)
- $^1/_2$ cup rice vinegar
- 1 teaspoon finely chopped garlic
- $^1/_4$ teaspoon sea salt

Combine ingredients in a jar and shake. This red chili vinegar can kept in the refrigerator for later use up to 3 months. ❖

Crispy Whole Chili and Chili Garlic Oil

❖ *Yields about $1^1/_4$ cups chili garlic oil*

- 1 cup virgin olive oil
- 1 cup dried whole Kee Noo, Chee Faar or Serrano chilies
- 1 tablespoon finely chopped garlic
- $^1/_4$ cup dried Kee Noo chili flakes
- 1 teaspoon sea salt

Place olive oil into a small deep skillet over medium low heat. Add dried whole chilies and fry until crisp. Remove crispy chilies and set aside to cool.

In the same oil add garlic and dried Kee Noo chili flakes and stir for 3 to 4 minutes. Remove oil from heat and let it cool completely, then place in a bottle with a lid. Chili oil is ready to be used as a dipping sauce or to make great dishes, and crispy whole chilies are ready to be eaten or added to other recipes. ❖

Cooked Basmati Rice

❖ *Makes about 6 cups*

$1^{2}/_{3}$ cups basmati rice	$2^{1}/_{4}$ cups water

Place Basmati rice and water into a small stockpot over high heat (a nonstick pot works best) and bring to a full boil. Stir rice to loosen it so that it doesn't stick to the bottom of the pot. Reduce heat to low and cover with a lid. Simmer rice for 17 minutes. Turn off heat and let rice stand undisturbed for 5 more minutes. Rice is ready to be eaten or used for other dishes. ❖

Cooked Long or Short Grain Brown Rice

❖ *Yields 6 cups*

1 cup brown rice	3 cups water

Place brown rice and water into a small stockpot (a nonstick pot works best) over high heat and bring to a boil. Reduce heat to low, cover with a lid and simmer for 24-25 minutes. Remove and set aside with the lid still on for 2-3 minutes. Cooked brown rice is ready to be eaten or used for other dishes. ❖

Cooked Thai Jasmine Rice (Thai Hom Mali Rice)

❖ *Makes about 6 cups*

2 cups Thai Jasmine rice	$2^{2}/_{3}$ cups water

Place rice and water in a small stockpot (a nonstick pot works best) over high heat and bring to a boil. It takes about 3-4 minutes to come to a boil. Stir rice to loosen it and prevent it from sticking to the bottom of the pot. Reduce heat to low and cover with a tight lid. Simmer the rice for 12 minutes, turn off the heat and let it stand undisturbed for 5 more minutes. Rice is ready to eat or for use in a stir-fry. ❖

Steamed Thai Sticky Rice

❖ *Makes about 4 cups*

2 cups Thai Sticky Rice (Thai Sweet Rice)	10 cups water in a steamer
3 cups boiling water	

A traditional way to cook sticky rice is to soak rice in cold water overnight or at least 3 hours, then steam over boiling water for 25 to 30 minutes.

For a quick method, soak rice in 3 cups of boiling water for 15 minutes. While rice is soaking, prepare steamer by putting 10 cups of water in the steamer and bringing it to a boil. Place a cloth napkin on steamer tray. Drain soaked rice through the napkin letting the soaking liquid drain into the bottom of the steamer. Fold the 4 sides of napkin to cover rice and put the lid on the steamer. Steam sticky rice for 20 minutes. Remove cooked rice from the steamer and it is ready to be eaten as part of a meal or used to prepare other dishes. ❖

Steamed Thai Black Rice

❖ *Makes about 4 cups*

- 2 cups Thai Black rice (Thai wild rice)
- 3 cups boiling water
- 10 cups water in a steamer

A traditional way to cook Thai black rice is to soak rice in cold water overnight, then steam over boiling water for 30 minutes.

For a quick method of preparing steamed Thai black rice:

Soak black rice in 3 cups of boiling water for 20 minutes. While rice is soaking, prepare steamer by putting 10 cups of water into the steamer and bringing to a boil. Place black or dark-colored cloth napkin on steamer tray (black rice will stain a white cloth). Drain soaked rice through the napkin into the water below, then fold the 4 sides to cover rice. Cover steamer with a lid and steam for 20 minutes. Remove cooked rice from steamer and rice is ready to be eaten or used to prepare other dishes. ❖

Crispy Shallots and Shallot Oil

- 2 cups Peeled and thinly sliced shallots
- $1^{1}/_{4}$ cups virgin olive oil

Place olive oil into a skillet over medium low heat. Add shallots and stir constantly for 6-8 minutes or until they turn crispy and golden brown. Make sure to rotate shallots into the middle of the skillet. (The sidewall of the skillet will overcook the shallots, if you do not rotate them.) Drain on paper towels and let them become absolutely cool before putting into a container with an airtight lid. Crispy shallots can keep for a month.

* Place cooled shallot olive oil into a bottle and keep refrigerated to use to make other great dishes. ❖

Crispy Garlic and Garlic Oil

- $1^{1}/_{2}$ cups virgin olive oil
- 1 cup garlic finely chopped or thinly sliced

Place 1 cup olive oil into a skillet over medium low heat. Add garlic and stir constantly to prevent garlic from sticking together. Stir for $2^{1}/_{2}$ to 3 minutes or until garlic turns golden brown. Turn off the heat and add remaining olive oil (this will stop garlic from overcooking). Drain and transfer crispy garlic to a pan lined with paper towels.

Let crispy garlic cool completely before transferring to an airtight jar with a lid. Crispy garlic can keep for up to 2 months.

Place cooled garlic oil into a bottle and keep refrigerated to use for other dishes. ❖

Crispy Ginger and Ginger Oil

2 cups peeled ginger very thinly sliced, in $1\frac{1}{2}$-2 inch strips

$1\frac{1}{4}$ cups virgin olive oil

Place virgin olive oil into a skillet over medium heat. Add ginger and stir constantly for 6-7 minutes or until it turns crispy and golden brown. Drain in a fine sieve, reserving oil, transfer ginger to a sheet pan lined with paper towels and allow it to become absolutely cool before you put it into a container with an airtight lid. (This will keep the ginger crispy and fresh for a couple months.) Place leftover ginger oil in a bottle and keep to use in other dishes. ❖

Crispy Leeks and Leek Oil

2 cups leeks, very thinly sliced in 3- $3\frac{1}{2}$ inch strips

$1\frac{1}{4}$ cups virgin olive oil

Place virgin olive oil in a skillet over medium heat. Add leeks and stir constantly for 3-4 minutes or until they turn crispy. Drain in a fine sieve and transfer crispy leeks to a sheet pan lined with paper towels. Allow them to become absolutely cool before you put them into a container with an airtight lid (this will keep the leeks crispy and fresh for a couple of weeks).

Place leftover leek olive oil in a bottle and keep in the refrigerator to use in other great dishes. ❖

Crispy Mee Krob Noodles

6 oz. Mee Krob Noodles

3 cups vegetable oil

Place oil into a deep skillet over medium high heat (to test oil, drop in a few strings of noodles, if they immediately puff and enlarge, oil is ready). Drop small amounts of noodles at a time into the hot oil, noodles should immediately puff. Remove noodles quickly and transfer to a paper towel-lined pan. Repeat with remaining noodles. Allow crispy noodles to cool completely before storing in a container with an airtight lid. ❖

Crispy Egg Noodles

1 lb. Small, thin or large fresh Egg Noodles

3 cups vegetable Oil

Place oil into a deep skillet over medium high heat (to test oil, drop in a few strings of Egg Noodles, if they puff and enlarge, oil is ready). Drop small amount of Egg Noodles at a time into the hot oil. Noodles should immediately puff. Turn noodles over quickly and transfer to a paper towel-lined pan. Repeat with remaining noodles. Allow Crispy Egg Noodles to cool completely before storing in a container with an airtight lid. Crispy Egg Noodles can be eaten as a snack or used to make great dishes. ❖

Crispy Wonton Strips

- 1 pack wonton Skins, cut into $^{1}/_{4}$ inch wide strips
- 2 cups vegetable oil

Place oil into a deep skillet over medium heat (test oil by putting a couple wonton strips in. If the strips puff right away, oil is ready to be used). Drop a small amount of Wonton Strips at a time into the hot oil and stir to prevent wontons from sticking together. Cook until wontons turn crispy and golden brown. Remove quickly to a paper towel lined pan. Repeat with the remaining wonton skins. Allow Crispy Wonton Strips to cool completely, and place them in a container with a tight lid. Crispy Wonton Strips can be eaten as a snack or used to make wonderful dishes. ❖

Crispy Silver Noodles

- 6 oz. Silver Noodles
- 3 cups vegetable oil

Place oil into a deep skillet over medium high heat (To test oil, drop in a few strings of noodles, if they immediately puff and enlarge, oil is ready.) Drop small amounts of noodles at a time into the hot oil, noodles should immediately puff. Remove noodles quickly and transfer to a paper towel-lined pan. Repeat with remaining noodles. Allow crispy noodles to cool completely before storing in a container with an airtight lid. ❖

Soft Pad Thai Noodles

- 12 oz. Pad Thai noodles
- 8 cups cold water

Place noodles into a large bowl. Add cold water and let it soak for 3 hours. Drain, set aside until completely air-dried before you use them.

For a quick way to prepare the noodles: **P**lace Pad Thai noodles into a large bowl. Add boiling enough water to cover noodles and stir with a fork to loosen up the noodles. Soak for 3 minutes. Drain and rinse with cold water and set aside until noodles are completely air dried before you use.

*Remember if you soak them for more than 3 minutes, the noodles will expand too much, get soggy and too soft for stir-fry. ❖

Soft Mee Krob Noodles

- 10 oz. Mee Krob noodles
- 8 cups cold water

Place noodles into a large bowl. Add cold water and let it soak for 3 to 4 hours, drain and set aside until completely air-dried before you use them.

For a quick way to prepare Soft Mee Krob noodles:

*P*lace Mee Krob noodles into a large bowl. Add enough boiling water to cover noodles and soak for 3 minutes. Stir with a fork to loosen up the noodles. Drain and rinse with cold water and set aside about an hour until noodles are completely air dried before you use them.

**R*emember, if you soak noodles in hot water for more than 3 minutes, the noodles will expand too much, get soggy, and will be too soft for stir-fry. ❖

Soft Silver Noodles

6 oz. Silver noodles	8 cups cold water

*P*lace noodles into a large bowl. Add cold water and let them soak for 3 hours, and drain. Soft silver noodles are ready to be used.

*F*or a quick way to prepare soft noodles:

*P*lace silver noodles into a large bowl. Add enough boiling water to cover noodles and soak for 2 minutes. Stir with a fork to loosen up the noodles. Drain and rinse with cold water and set aside until ready to use.

*Remember if you soak silver noodles in hot water for more than 2 minutes, the noodles will expand too much, get soggy and be too soft for stir-frying. ❖

Soft Rad-Na Noodles

12 oz. dried Rad-Na noodles	8 cups fresh water

*P*lace water into a medium stockpot over high heat and bring to a boil. Add dried Rad-Na noodles and cook for 8 to 9 minutes. Remove, strain and rinse in cold water until noodles cool and let air-dry before use. Rad-Na noodles are used to make Chow Fun, noodle soup and of course, Rad-Na noodles with any variety of sauces.

**R*emember, if you cook too long, the noodles will expand too much, get soggy, the it doesn't taste good and is too soft for stir-fry. ❖

Vegetable Stock

❖ *Makes about 6 cups*

12 cups water	1 large brown onion, cut into half with skin on
2 long celery stalks, cut into 4 sections	4 Cilantro roots, or 10 sprigs cilantro or parsley
2 large Carrots, cut into 4 sections	

*P*lace water into a medium stockpot over high heat and bring to a boil. Add remaining ingredients and bring to a boil again. Reduce heat to low and simmer for about 45 minutes to 1 hour. Strain and it is ready to be used or let it cool and keep in the refrigerator for later use. Freeze for longer storage. Freeze stock in one cup units in plastic containers with tight lids. This will make it easier when you need them for later use. ❖

Lemongrass Stock

❖ *Makes about 6 cups*

- 12 cups water
- 2 Stalks fresh lemongrass or 1/2 cup dried lemongrass (do not use lemongrass powder to make stock)
- 4 pieces dried galanga or fresh galanga
- 6 whole fresh or dried Kaffir lime leaves
- 1 medium brown onion, cut in half with skin on
- 1 large carrot cut into 4 sections
- 1 long celery stick cut into 4 sections

Bring water to a boil in a large stockpot over high heat. Add remaining ingredients and return to a boil. Reduce heat to medium (just at the boiling point) and boil until stock is reduced by half, about 45 minutes to 1 hour. Strain stock and let cool before refrigerating for later use. Lemongrass stock can keep in the refrigerator for up to a week, or freeze it for longer storage.

To find out when the stock has reduced by half, use a stick, measure the level of water with all ingredients already in the stockpot and mark with a string or rubber band, then move string to half point. There you have it, stock reduced by half. ❖

Simple Vegetable Soup

❖ *Recipe serves 2 to 4*

- 4 cups chicken or vegetable stock (see page198)
- 1 tablespoon Thai fish sauce seasoning
- 1/2 tablespoon Thai light soy sauce
- 2 tablespoons cilantro or Italian parsley leaves
- 1/4 teaspoon ground white pepper
- 1 tablespoon finely cut chives or 2 tablespoons sliced scallions

Bring stock to a boil in a stockpot over high heat. Remove and put in a large soup bowl. Add remaining ingredients and serve. This is a quick bowl of soup when you just want something simple. You may add cooked Jasmine rice or soft noodles to make a heart healthy meal. (I do this quite often for myself.) ❖

Simple Couscous

❖ *Yields about 6 cups*

- 1 1/2 cups medium coarse Couscous
- 2 3/4 cups boiling Lemongrass or vegetable stock

Place Couscous into an 8 by 12 inch deep tray or bowl. Add boiling lemongrass or vegetable stock, cover tightly with plastic wrap and set aside for 1/2 hour. Couscous is ready to be used to make other great dishes. ❖

Tamarind Juice

❖ *Makes about 2 cups tamarind juice*

1/4 cup wet tamarind paste	2 cups cold water

Combine water and tamarind paste in a medium bowl and squeeze with your hands for 2 minutes until paste loosens and disperses through the water. Let it soak for 30 minutes, then strain through a fine sieve. Tamarind juice can be kept in the refrigerator up to 5 days or frozen for longer storage. To freeze tamarind juice, place in an empty ice tray and freeze in the freezer compartment. Remove the frozen tamarind cubes and transfer to a plastic bag or container. This will make it easy when you need them later. ❖

Tomato Purée

❖ *Recipe makes about 5 cups*

8 cups water	6 cloves garlic peeled
12 large tomatoes	

Place water into a medium stockpot over high heat and bring to a boil. Cut shallow cross in the bottom end of each tomato, opposite the stem side. Drop tomatoes into boiling water and blanch for 2 minutes. Remove and transfer to a large bowl of cold water to stop cooking process. Peel and seed tomatoes over a bowl to catch seeds and water. Strain the tomato seeds and water in a fine sieve and reserve tomato water for purée.

Place tomatoes, garlic, salt and reserved tomato water into a blender and blend until smooth. Transfer purée to a medium stockpot and bring to a boil over high heat. Reduce heat to low and simmer for 20 minutes, remove and let it cool. Tomato purée can be kept in the refrigerator up to 10 days; freeze for longer storage. Store purée in one-cup size plastic containers with tight lids. ❖

Red Bell Pepper Purée

❖ *Recipe makes about 4 cups*

12 large red bell peppers	6 cloves garlic, peeled
1 teaspoon sea salt	

Roast red bell peppers on a wire rack over a gas burner at medium heat or under broiler until blistered on all sides, turning frequently. Transfer to a paper or plastic bag, close, and let stand at least 15 to 20 minutes. Peel and seed pepper over a large mixing bowl to catch the pepper liquid, strain the liquid and set aside.

Place roasted, peeled, seeded pepper, pepper liquid, garlic and salt into a blender and purée until smooth. Transfer purée to a medium deep saucepan and bring to a boil over medium heat. Reduce heat to low and simmer for 15 to 20 minutes. Cooled puree can be kept in refrigerator up to a week; freeze for longer storage. Store purée in one-cup size plastic containers with tight lids. ❖

Sweet Basil
Mint leaves
Meng-Luck Basil
Puk-Boong
Cilantro (Puk-Chee)
Cilantro roots (Rark Puk-Chee)
Lemongrass
Thai Long String Bean
Chives Flower
Bamboo Shoots
Green Eggplant
Green Papaya & Banana Blossom
Ginger (Khing)
Galanga (Kha)
Kaffir Lime Leaves

Garlic , Shallots & Dried Chilies

Pomelo

Mangosteen

Kee-Noo Chilies

Star fruit

Custard Apple

Galingale (Kra-Chay)

Chom Poo

Langsat

Mango

Rambutan

Lum Yai

Tamarind

Lychee

Salak

● Felt great.... elephant camp in Chiang Mai.

Golden Memories

Riding in a howdah on the back of a gentle but enormous elephant — swaying from side to side with each step up a mountain trail through banana plantations and teak jungles. Rewarding your animal at the end of the trek with bananas and sugar cane. Meeting hilltribe members who serve tea in bamboo cups, then dance and demonstrate crossbow target shooting. Stopping at a roadside stand to buy roasted coconuts — the milk a smoky delicacy — the flesh peeling easily from the skin.

A bamboo raft ride down a river, spotting mother and baby elephants on the shore. Eating unripe mango salad in a spacious home built entirely out of teak. Speculating upon the whereabouts of the missing Jim Thompson, a silk trader who disappeared 30 years ago. The Grand Palace in Bangkok with its incredible richness of design and ornamentation. Thai people with ever-present smiles — warm and sincere. The overwhelming traffic of Bangkok versus the tranquility of Chiang Mai and its temples. Orange-robed Buddhist monks sweeping temple steps or repairing temple walls and doorways.

Celebrating the King's birthday, along with the rest of Thailand, by lighting yellow candles at 7:30 p.m. and singing the Thai version of "Happy Birthday, Dear King." These are but a few golden memories. What a magnificent land is... Thailand.

Linda K. Mundel

● **This is how the famous Thai's silk begin.**

Glossary of Ingredients

Bamboo shoots: available canned in various forms — whole, in chunks, sliced, shredded, and in strips. I find the sliced and strips easiest to use and easy to find in all Asian and other supermarkets.

Basil, Thai: called Bai Hua Ra Pha in Thai, darker in color, stronger in aroma, and spicier in flavor than regular basil, but otherwise interchangeable with it. A sprig of the basil flowers makes a nice garnish.

Basil, Holy: called Bai Kra Prao in Thai, 2 kinds, red and white (we call it white, but actually it is green) that are used in cooking. I prefer the white variety; this basil has a great flavor and a spiritual scent. When you taste it, you'll be hooked on it.

Basil, Meng Luck: this basil is very hard to find in the US, you can find it at Thai markets but only in the summer season. It doesn't grow in a cold climate unless you use a plant light bulb. The flavor tastes like medicine, but tasty medicine, and has a strong aroma.

Bean condiment, Salted soybean: these are the same product with different brands and names. Thai or Chinese varieties are similar; use either. Made from fermented soybeans, this salty condiment combines with other ingredients to create a complex, subtle flavor. Add to stir fry rice noodles or as part of dipping sauce ingredients.

Chili paste, fresh ground red: gives a spicy, hot flavor. Also known by its Indonesian name, Sambal Oelek. Combine with vinegar to use as seasoning and add to noodle dishes.

Chili paste, Roasted: important for soups in particular, as well as for many sauces and salad dressings. Made from a combination of ingredients (typically roasted red chilies, garlic, onion, dried shrimp, sugar, fish sauce, and vegetable oil), the paste gives a distinctively tangy, mildly smoky flavor.

Chilies Kee Noo: this tiny green or red Thai variety may be very hot, but unlike other kinds of chilies, Kee Noo chilies impart a great flavor and satisfaction even when your mouth is on fire and you sweat like you just came out of a hot sauna. Also known as Thai birdseye chilies.

Chilies, Serrano: small, green, and semi-hot. Jalapenos or other similar hot chilies can be readily substituted. Be careful never to touch your eyes after handling chilies, because the pungent oils will burn them.

Curry paste, Green: this combination of fresh green chilies, lemon grass, cilantro root, and galangal has a spicy, refreshing flavor.

Curry paste, Mussamun: an aromatic combination of cardamom, lemon grass, cinnamon, cloves, and chilies. This curry is great for lamb.

Curry paste, Panang: This is a combination of dried red chilies, shallots, Kaffir lime rinds, galangal, lemon grass, garlic, coriander, cumin, salt and shrimp paste and coarsely pounded. Panang curry paste can be used to sauté meat and vegetables, make curry sauce, risotto and pasta sauce.

Curry paste, Red: similar to Panang curry paste.

Daikon sprouts: these long, slim sprouts have the spicy flavor of radish. Use in sushi rolls, in salads, and for garnish.

Firm brown tofu: the flavor resembles baked beans, this is used in Pad Thai noodles. Tofu (also known as bean curd) comes in many varieties, but the firm brown kind is always in 3-inch by $^{1}/_{2}$-inch thick squares. I also like to use soft tofu to make soup and stir-fry spicy tofu, Chinese style.

Fish sauce, Thai: the basic most essential Thai seasoning, this is a salty, very aromatic liquid that provides a distinctive flavor. You can cook Thai food anywhere in the world, never leave home without it.

Galangal: also known as galingale, kha, and laos, this is a root resembling ginger, but with a distinctive flavor, a more translucent skin, and a tinge of pink when fresh. The flavor is stronger than ginger and it is used in Tom Yum Soup (hot and sour soup), Tom Kha Soup (coconut milk soup) and in lemon grass stock.

Green mango: unripe mango can be used just like green apple; substitute the apple if necessary. Thailand has hundreds of varieties of mango. Some mangos are better to eat green and some are good when eaten fully ripe. The most famous Thai dessert is sweet ripe mango with coconut sticky rice. I prefer to have green mango with a dipping sauce, a combination of sea salt, palm sugar, and Kee Noo chilies.

Green papaya: tart and crunchy green papaya is used mainly in Thai Papaya Salad and ripe papaya is used to make sauce or eaten as a dessert or snack.

Kaffir lime leaves: glossy, dark green leaves of the Kaffir lime tree; they impart a refreshing, mysterious lemon-lime flavor. When my daughters Aisha or Chyna have a stomachache, I always make Kaffir lime tea with honey and a little sea salt and it's always done the trick.

Kra-Shy: a long, slender root, related to ginger, with a flavor that suggests a combination of ginger, turmeric, and galangal. It is sometimes available fresh or frozen in Thai markets.

Lemon grass: indispensable in Thai cooking, this consists of long, very firm stalks with green tops. The grass has a pronounced lemon flavor and aroma. The stalks will last up to a couple of months in the refrigerator, and an average-size stalk yields about 4 tablespoons chopped. Dried lemon grass is also available.

Manila clams: most Manila (Malaysian) clams are farm raised. They are the sweetest, and tenderest clams I've ever tasted, and tend to be not at all gritty.

Mushrooms, Enoki: these pure white mushrooms have long, skinny stems and tiny caps. They're beautiful to look at in sushi stuffing, salads, sautés, and soups, and they have a delicate buttery flavor.

Mushrooms, Shiitake: fresh or dried, exceptionally meaty and flavorful mushrooms of which only the caps are used. Great either steamed or sautéed.

Noodles, Mee-Krob: very thin dried rice noodles, known in Thai as Sen-Mee, other Asians call them Mai-Fun or Bihon. This noodle is wheat-free and comparable in thickness to angel hair pasta.

Noodles, Pad Thai: dried rice noodles, known in Thai as Sen-Chan. I've called it Pad Thai noodles after the most famous noodles in Thailand and abroad because it is easy to remember. They are available in narrow, medium, and wide versions. I prefer the medium ones, which are about the width of linguine.

Noodles, Rad Na: dried or fresh, these are called Hor-Fhun in Cantonese, similar to regular Western noodles, but made with rice flour. Because fresh rice noodles are already steam-cooked when you buy them, they cook very quickly. Purchase only what you need; even in the refrigerator they only last two or three days. The fresh Rad-Na is available in most Asian markets or you can find a dried variety (see how to use it in the Basic Easy Recipes chapter) in supermarkets made by 7 Lotus brand.

Nori: dark green or black sheets of dried Japanese or other Asian seaweed, used for wrapping sushi, in soup or as a garnish.

Oyster sauce: this combination of oyster extract, soy sauce, and starch has a mildly salty fishy flavor. It is a Chinese condiment commonly available in all Asian and other supermarkets.

Palm sugar: a coarse brown sugar that is crystallized from the sap of the coconut palm. It is collected much like the sap of maple trees, but the workers have to shinny all the way up to the tops of the palms to do it. The sugar lends a sweet, fruity flavor. If unavailable, substitute with honey.

Panang curry paste: the most versatile of all curry pastes; this is a mix of red chilies, onion, garlic, galangal, lemongrass, and kaffir lime. It has a wonderfully interesting complex flavor.

Pickled ginger: a hot, sweet-tart condiment that is served with sushi and to refresh the palate between courses.

Plum sauce: a fruity, translucent, sweet-sour sauce that is common in Chinese cooking. Use as a dip for egg rolls, wonton, duck, and many other dishes.

Rice vinegar: a clear, pale straw color, and milder than cider or wine vinegar.

Salt Free Thai seasoning, Tommy Tang's Brand: a combination of garlic, black pepper, white pepper, chili powder, and cayenne pepper. At the restaurant we use this in almost every marinade and in many sauces. Or try brushing French bread with olive oil, sprinkling on the seasoning, and baking it as you would garlic bread — it's fantastic.

Santa Fe chili powder: rosy red, with a sweet, spicy flavor superior to that of regular chili powder.

Sausage, Thai: the same as Chinese sausage, this is a firm pork sausage that resembles a small salami. Made with pork or pork and liver, they are available regular, fatty, or extra-lean.

Sesame oil, Asian: brown, aromatic oil made from roasted sesame seeds. Don't substitute with the clear, unroasted sesame oil available in natural food stores; it doesn't have the same rich fragrance or nutty flavor.

Shrimp powder: made from small shrimp that are dried and coarsely ground; the name "powder" is really a misnomer, but that is how the product is usually labeled. The flavor resembles shrimp in the same way that the flavor of beef jerky resembles beef.

Skins, Egg-roll: paper-thin squares or rounds made from wheat flour; similar to wonton wrappers.

Skins or wrapper, Spring roll: are similar to egg roll skins, but thinner, round or square and made from rice flour instead of wheat.

Sugarcane juice: pressed from sugarcane, this sweet liquid can be drunk by itself or added to recipes for marinade and sauce.

Tamarind juice: a very sour liquid extracted from tamarind paste or the pod of the tamarind tree. If unavailable, substitute half the amount of lemon juice.

Thin soy sauce: made from yellow soybeans, this is lighter and less salty than regular soy sauce. I prefer to use 7 Lotus or Golden Boat brand which has no MSG or preservatives.

Wasabi: dried, powdered, green Japanese horseradish, used to give pungency to sushi. Use sparingly; it's extremely hot.

Wrappers, Pot-sticker: this thin round dough is made from either rice or wheat flour.

Wrappers, Wonton: dough squares made from wheat flour and starch; slightly thicker than egg-roll skins. ❖

● I'm hungry.